W9-BMT-910

HELP AMERICA READ

A Handbook for Volunteers

Gay Su Pinnell
and
Irene C. Fountas

HEINEMANN
Portsmouth, NH

Heinemann
A division of Reed Elsevier Inc.
361 Hanover Street
Portsmouth, NH 03801-3912

Offices and agents throughout the world

Copyright © 1997 by Gay Su Pinnell and Irene C. Fountas

All rights reserved. No part of this book may be reproduced in any form or by any electronic or mechanical means, including information storage and retrieval systems, without permission in writing from the publisher, except by a reviewer, who may quote brief passages in a review.

Library of Congress Cataloging-in-Publication Data
CIP is on file with the Library of Congress.
ISBN 0-435-07250-1

Editor: Lois Bridges
Production: Renée Le Verrier and Melissa L. Inglis
Cover design: Barbara Werden
Text design: Darci Mehall
Manufacturing: Louise Richardson

Cover photos by Vicki Kasabian, Irene C. Fountas, and Joel Brown

Printed in the United States of America on acid-free paper
01 00 99 98 97   ML   1 2 3 4 5 6 7 8 9

We dedicate this book to all
volunteers who give unselfishly to
our children and our community.

CONTENTS

In the United States today, literacy is a vital individual and national need. If children aren't reading and writing by third grade, their future academic and economic success may be jeopardized and even diminished. Our goal is strong literacy for all children by the end of third grade, a goal that demands an intensive instructional effort in kindergarten, first, and second grades. Volunteers play a key role in guaranteeing successful literacy for all children. We must, therefore, have high expectations for ourselves as literacy volunteers as well as for the children with whom we work.

This book is for all literacy volunteers dedicated to helping young children in schools, libraries, community and daycare centers, businesses, shelters, churches and synagogues, youth service groups, and local literacy projects. Indeed, the book will help all who want to help children—teacher education students who are just beginning their careers in education, paraprofessional assistants inside schools, and parents who are working with their children at home.

We offer ten recommendations for working with children in reading and writing. We hope that you enjoy them all and experience the pleasure of seeing children grow and change as they gain in ability and confidence. The benefits for children are clear. And there are rich rewards for you as well—the deep satisfaction and joy of helping children into the promising world of literacy.

ACKNOWLEDGMENTS

We acknowledge those individuals who, with their vision, expertise, and commitment realized the potential of literacy volunteers and emphasized the importance of their contributions: Uri Treisman, who involved us in the study of how literacy volunteers can serve children, and Mike Gibbons of Heinemann, who saw the need for a handbook and a guide for coordinators. We especially acknowledge our colleagues Diane DeFord, Sue Constable, Colleen Griffiths, and Janet George, whose exemplary work with AmeriCorps members has inspired us and who contribute to volunteerism through their work every day. They have given unselfishly of their time and talent to help young children learn to read.

Additionally, we want to thank Andrea McCarrier, Justina Henry, Mary Fried, Joan Wiley, Sue Hundley, Diane Powell, Carol Lyons, Diane DeFord, and others who provide leadership for the Early Literacy Learning Initiative, which has helped us learn so much from teachers and children. Their work exemplifies the partnerships that are necessary if all children are to become literate.

Our office staff, too, have helped to make possible the two volumes, *Help America Read: A Handbook for Volunteers* and *A Coordinator's Guide to Help America Read*. Polly Taylor has assisted in hundreds of ways to prepare the manuscript; Heather Kroll, Erika Hession, Jennifer Warner, and Karen Travelo provided valuable assistance in preparing the illustrations and supporting documents.

Ron Melhado, Bill Wayson, and Elfrieda Pinnell provided their assistance, encouragement, and loving patience at critical times in our work, and for that we are truly grateful.

Special thanks is expressed here to the staff at Heinemann, who worked to meet deadlines and create high quality volumes that will be useful to volunteers and others. Renée Le Verrier's expertise and enthusiasm, Mike Gibbons' encouragement and confidence, and Melissa Inglis' meticulous attention to details and presentation were significant contributions to the work. It could not have been completed without them. We are deeply indebted to our editor, Lois Bridges, who worked unceasingly, gave of her many talents, and was a true partner in this work.

We also recognize and express our appreciation to enlightened community leaders who see the need for this work. In particular, the Charles A. Dana Foundation, The Martha Holden Jennings Foundation, and the Noyce Foundation have, over the years, consistently supported teachers and children in literacy efforts such as Reading Recovery, The Early Literacy Learning Initiative, and AmeriCorps for Math and Literacy. These leadership efforts, supported and guided by service oriented foundations, have provided a resource for the work in *Help America Read: A Handbook for Volunteers* and *A Coordinator's Guide to Help America Read*.

Most of all we thank those who will use these volumes—the volunteers who give of their time, expecting only the reward of children's joy in learning; and those who lead and coordinate volunteer efforts so that they can succeed in this important task. We thank you for your time and your caring, and we wish you the many rewards of your work.

Congratulations! You have made an important decision to help children with one of the greatest challenges they will ever face—the challenge of learning to read and write. It is an exciting challenge and, with the right support from a caring adult, children can learn to read and write easily and joyfully. All young children want to become literate. You will play a key role in their literacy learning as you show them you believe in their ability and success.

As a literacy volunteer, you provide the extra time and individual attention children need to learn all about our most useful lifetime skills—reading and writing. With your help, they'll grow to appreciate the significance of literacy in their own lives and all the many different ways reading and writing can both serve and delight them.

You will also learn and benefit from your work with children. Volunteers often describe the excitement of watching a young child learn. And just think—the child you help today can do more to help others in the future—sometimes immediately. Often, when children learn to read and write at school, they go home and read and write with their younger brothers and sisters. We have even known young children to take their reading books home and show a family member how to read.

When you volunteer, you give your most valuable resource—time. Because your time is precious to both you and the children, our goal is to help you be as productive and efficient as possible. In this book we explain specific ways to guide a young child's successful journey into literacy. We also show you how to organize your work plans and tutoring materials. At the end of each chapter, in a feature we call *Take Note*, we invite you to reflect on your work with children. In this way, we hope to support you as an effective literacy volunteer who can make a world of difference for a young child.

Let's Get Started!

No matter where you serve—a school, public library, community agency, church, synagogue, or afternoon learning center—your goal is to be a successful literacy volunteer. Success is easy to define. It means that you:

- Work effectively with children.
- Blend comfortably into the setting where you are working.
- Manage your volunteer position so that it fits well into your own life.

Being a literacy volunteer for young children is most rewarding. You'll enjoy it to the fullest when it's manageable and efficient.

GETTING TO KNOW WHERE YOU WORK

Every time you enter a setting as a volunteer, you enter as a guest. We offer a few tips to help you work effectively so you won't have to rely exclusively on help from the busy personnel. Though we emphasize schools, these ideas apply to other settings as well.

First, get to know where you work. You will feel more comfortable and do a better job if you know your way around. The volunteer coordinator may give you an orientation tour, but if you are working on your own, just ask for directions. For example, if applicable, you might ask:

- Where are the office, the library, the restrooms, and the cafeteria?

- Where are the fire exits and what are the emergency procedures?

- What do signals such as bells or buzzers mean?

- Where are the parking areas and what are the regulations?

In a school, the principal oversees all operations. Always be cautious and check with the teacher or school principal if you need to make an important or unusual decision. For example, do not give medication of any kind to a child. Instead, consult the principal or the school nurse.

In other settings, learn who's in charge. When in doubt, check with that person. Most programs are managed by an individual who is designated as the coordinator, liaison, or contact person for volunteers. Be sure that you know who that person is and how to contact him or her.

Working independently in the classroom

While teachers value and welcome volunteers, it's a challenge to find extra time to plan and talk with their classroom volunteers. Once you have general directions from the teacher, try to carry out your volunteer responsibilities with a minimum of assistance. Here are some suggestions that will make that possible:

- Set up a regular work schedule so that neither you nor the teacher has to spend much time arranging your work each week. It's often best to record your schedule on a calendar that you can both easily access.

- Ask for a copy of the classroom rules and any special management procedures so that your message to the children is consistent (just in case they ask you for permission to do something the teacher doesn't permit).

- Find a place to keep and organize your tutoring materials (books, writing materials, cut-out pictures from magazines, etc.).

- Ask the teacher to assign children to work with you. Also ask the teacher to advise you on the assistance the children need most.

- Find the best place to work in an uninterrupted way with one child.

- Design a communication system (such as a clipboard or notepad) so that you and the teacher can write notes to each other.

- Create a system for notifying each other of absences so the teacher can let you know when your partner is absent, and you can let the teacher know when you are going to miss a day.

If you are working in a community center or daycare center, you may need to establish a small literacy area where you can work. The "tool kit" described in Chapter 12 is a way to store and organize your materials if you have no permanent space to work.

MEETING YOUR PARTNER

As a volunteer you may help in many ways, but none will be more reward-ing than working with an individual child. You may come to know one or more children very well during your time of service. Meeting your young partner for the first time is an exciting experience. Here are some ideas to help you both enjoy your first meeting.

- Tell your partner your name and write it for him[1] on a special card. (Most children in schools address all adults by Mr., Mrs., or Ms., but some settings are less formal and permit a first name basis.)

- Ask your partner's name and be sure to get the correct pronunciation. Some children may prefer their nickname.

- Avoid overwhelming your partner with too much talk, even though you'll want to invite him to talk and share just as much as he wants. For some children, especially those unaccustomed to a lot of talk in their own homes or communities, a rush of conversation is intimidating.

- Invite the child to listen to a good book that you read aloud. This will make your first meeting special. Choose something short that invites the child's interaction.

- Consider writing your schedule for your partner. You can make a book-mark with a clock or other figure to keep track of your time together. Explain to your partner the dates and times you will come, where you will work, and what you will do together.

- Discuss how you will notify the child when you are forced to miss a meeting so that he knows what to expect. When you are unable to at-tend your volunteer session, the child is disappointed. Advance notice helps.

Always respect your partner's confidentiality. Do not discuss the child, his work, his achievement record, or any other information of a personal nature with anyone but the child's teacher or your volunteer coordinator. You can, of course, tell your family or friends about an interesting or excit-ing moment in your work with your partner, but leave personal details out of the conversation. Whenever you talk about your children or their homes, always be positive.

Setting expectations

In general, your positive outlook will make you a successful volunteer. Know in your own mind that all children can learn and make it clear to your partner that he *cannot* fail. Express your confidence in him. Praise

---

[1]Whenever possible, we have used plural pronouns to avoid sexist language. When unable to avoid singular pronouns, we have alternated the masucline and the feminine from chapter to chapter.

him for specific accomplishments, and help him learn that he will succeed every time you work together.

While you want your partner to feel comfortable with you, you also want to establish that you are in charge. You set the tone and expectations for your work together. Be kind but firm. Do not say, "Would you like to . . . ?", which may inspire the child to exclaim, "No!" Instead, say with excitement, "Let's . . . !" Your partner will follow your lead. We help children build a sense of accomplishment not by letting them do whatever they want but by encouraging them to read and write and praising them for their specific efforts.

Building your relationship

Your positive relationship with your partner lies at the heart of your volunteer work. It's not so much the specific activities you do with your partner but the enjoyment and success he'll come to associate with reading and writing that really count. How can you create a warm and caring relationship with your partner?

- Work out a signal (such as a light touch on the shoulder or a simple wave) to get his attention each time you arrive in the classroom. He should know to come right away (unless he is involved in a reading group or other instructional situation that the teacher would not want him to leave) and begin work with you immediately.

- Spend a few minutes just chatting quietly. How is he? What has he been doing since you saw him last? Does he have anything to share with you? Perhaps he's found a book he'd like to show you!

- Introduce a book that you are going to read to him by telling him why you chose it especially for him.

- Add small gestures of friendship that make a big difference. Anything you have with the child's name on it (such as a Post-it on the book you are going to read) will signal that you are thinking of him.

- Make a list of the books that you read together (see Chapter 4). Add to it each time you share a book together. In this way, you can show him how much reading he is doing.

- Complete your volunteer work for the year by designing a special certificate for your partner that celebrates the learning time you spent together.

MANAGING YOUR TIME

Make sure that your volunteer time is time well spent. Think carefully about your own schedule and the time you can devote to working with young children. It's better to meet realistic goals than to over-promise and fall short of your commitment. Here are some suggestions to help you manage your time:

- Choose a location for volunteer work that is convenient for you. If you have to drive out of your way, it will be harder to complete your volunteer schedule.

- Carefully consider your weekly schedule. List everything that you are expected to do. How much time can you realistically devote to volunteering? Make your commitment and write your volunteer time in on your schedule.

- Read this handbook so that you understand what you are trying to accomplish and how best to accomplish it. Many volunteer programs will train you.

- Gather your tutoring materials and organize them so that you are ready to go.

- Establish good communication with the people in the community center, church, or school where you are volunteering.

- After you have volunteered for a month or so, talk with the teacher and coordinator and make adjustments as needed. At that point, you will have a better idea of what's possible.

You'll find every hour you spend working with your partner rewarding, and your work will give him the gift of literacy. Make the most of your time so you can continue your valuable work.

TAKE NOTE

From time to time, it will help to reflect on your work as a literacy volunteer. What worked well? What didn't work as well? What might you do next time to be more successful? Consider the questions we've listed below as you reflect on your new work as a literacy volunteer:

- ◆ Do I know the layout of the place where I work?
- ◆ Am I familiar with the operating and safety procedures?
- ◆ Have I met the people in charge and those with whom I will work closely?
- ◆ Have I begun to create a trusting relationship with my partner so he knows my expectations and we cheerfully accomplish our tutoring goals for each session?
- ◆ Am I creating a plan that will help me conduct an effective session with minimal disruption to the place where I volunteer?
- ◆ Am I keeping a record of each completed session so that I can review it and improve the next session?
- ◆ Have I worked out ways to manage my own time so that I can enjoy my volunteer work with children?

CHAPTER **TWO**

Ten Ways to Help

No doubt you are asking yourself, "How exactly do I help my young partner learn to read and write?" We have ten recommendations for you. Try them in any order; they aren't sequential. They're all enjoyable, and each one will help you help your partner learn to read and write.

I. TALKING WITH CHILDREN

Children learn to talk by talking. The more they talk, particularly with an adult, the more language they learn. They discover new words and new ways of using those words to express themselves. A strong foundation in spoken language helps children read and write. Children who like to talk tend to be strong readers and writers. You can help your young partner become a stronger reader and writer just by talking with her—sharing everyday conversation about what she likes to eat, play, or do on the weekends.

2. READING TO CHILDREN

Can you guess the one most important way you can help children into literacy? It begins with a good book and ends with a contented child. There's no better way to help a child than to read her a good book—unless, of course, you read her two, three, or four good books! Reading aloud is especially important for those children who've not had many read-aloud experiences at home. Look for wonderful books to read out loud (and we offer many suggestions for good books throughout this book and in the appendices). Discover new books together or reread old favorites.

And don't forget to invite your partner to join in the reading, too. Children need to understand that when they open up a book, the language they encounter will sound a little different than the talk they are accustomed to hearing. How do children learn this? It's easy! They learn from hearing lots and lots of stories read aloud. As you read to your partner, she'll discover that the language inside books has a special way of sounding. It's not just talk written down. To become successful readers, all children need to understand this difference.

3. READING WITH CHILDREN (SHARED READING)

Think about how you learned to ride a bike. Some kind and patient person (your mother, father, big brother) held onto the bike and ran along beside you while you pedaled for all you were worth. Eventually you got the feel of the bike on the open road and you were off, riding as though there were no tomorrow. That's what shared reading is all about. Instead of holding onto a bike, you hold onto a book. You and the child read the story at the same time. You both look at the print while you point to the words. Your partner gets a feel for reading and before you know it, she's off in a book and reading on her own.

4. HELPING CHILDREN READ ON THEIR OWN

Practice makes perfect and learning to read is no exception. Children need a lot of practice reading. You can contribute in a big way to children's literacy development by simply listening and helping them as they read aloud to you. Children read aloud to their teachers during classroom instruction, but they also need many chances to read to a good listener. What do you do? Invite your partner to read to you. Listen carefully and offer her help when she has trouble.

5. WRITING FOR CHILDREN

It's no surprise that we often learn best from watching someone do what we want to learn how to do. We learn how to crack an egg by watching our dad tackle Saturday morning breakfast. We learn how to change a tire by watching our uncle wrestle with a flat. And we master the utility and beauty of writing by watching a writer at work. When you write for your partner, talk with her and decide together what to write—names, labels, or stories—and then write it. It often helps to "think out loud" about the writing process, detailing what you are doing for your partner as you do it ("Let's see, I'm going to add a new word, so I leave a space here and . . ."). Once you've finished your writing, you read it out loud, read it with your partner, and then invite her to read it alone. In this way, you gently ease your partner into writing on her own.

6. WRITING WITH CHILDREN (SHARED WRITING)

Writing *with* children ups the ante a bit. Instead of doing all the writing for your partner, you invite her to share the writing with you. In fact, this approach, sometimes called "shared writing," gives the child a chance to do some of the writing while you fill in the rest. This is how it works: You and your partner decide together what to write and then you "share the pen" as you write the message. You can tackle all the hard parts and let your partner handle the easier parts. You can then read the message you wrote, or invite the child to read it, or read it together.

7. HELPING CHILDREN WRITE ON THEIR OWN

Think about all the decisions that writing entails. You have to decide what to write about, how to write it, what words to choose, how to spell the words, and so on and so on. Even the simplest writing can involve dozens of decisions—and that's a lot of decision making for a brand new writer. That's where you come in. You can make it possible for the child to write on her own. Your partner thinks of what to write and begins to write it; you help as needed. You can then help her pick up a few new skills each time you work together: how to spell common words such as *the* or *what*, the right place to put a period, and how to begin proper names with a capital letter.

8. UNDERSTANDING PHONICS, LETTERS, AND WORDS

Did you ever stop to consider that before you were a reader, you probably didn't know that language is made up of individual words, sounds, and letters? Helping children understand the special features of written language or print has a lot to do with learning how to read—and a lot to do with "phonics." Phonics is a teaching method that helps children learn how sounds and letters relate to each other. Children can use this knowledge to figure out new words while they are reading. Children learn that words are made up of sounds and that some words sound like other words (at the beginning, at the end, and in the middle). They also learn what individual letters look like and how to tell one letter from another. As you help children write words and work with tools such as magnetic letters, you can help them unravel the mysteries of letters, sounds, and words.

9. MAKING BOOKS

The only pleasure greater than reading a book, possibly, is writing your own. And it turns out that writing a book challenges children to use all their literacy skills. Book making combines all or any of the ways of working with children in reading and writing. We're not talking *War and Peace*, of course. The book your partner makes will be very simple—often just one line of print per page. But what joy! The child becomes the author of her own little book that she can keep and read again and again—to you, her neighbor, her teacher, her classmates, her sister, her brother . . . you get the idea!

10. CONNECTING WITH CHILDREN'S HOMES

We hear it all the time. "Education should be a shared endeavor between home and school." We agree, but how do we make that happen? It's not as difficult as it might sound. For one thing, children love to talk, especially about the exciting things they've done while away from their families. After an exciting session with you, you can bet that your partner will return home and report to her family members what you talked about, the books she read with you, and the writing you did together. But you can also directly influence the reading and writing she does at home by sending home reading and writing materials. When she arrives home with a blank book to fill with her own words and pictures, her family will know she's on her way to becoming a real reader and writer.

These are our ten recommendations for helping children become readers and writers. Each chapter of this handbook develops in detail each recommendation for helping children learn to read and write, so you'll know exactly what to do and why to do it. Sometimes you'll want to step in and give the child a lot of support. And other times you'll want to pull back and let her take off flying down the road to literacy on her own. Keep in mind what it takes to learn to ride a bike. Once you know how to balance and pedal and steer, you don't want anyone holding on. You want to do it yourself! But you certainly enjoy having a friend along to share the ride. Learning to read and write is a lot like learning how to ride a bike.

WORKING WITH ENGLISH LEARNERS

You may work with a child who doesn't speak English at home. Speaking more than one language is a gift, not a deficit. You'll want to encourage young children to be proud of their language abilities. We refer to children who are learning the English language as "English learners." How can you determine how much English a child knows? You will learn more about the level of English a child can speak and understand as you talk with her. You'll also want to ask the child's teacher and others who know the child well.

At first, a child who doesn't speak much English may be very quiet. But she still enjoys—and needs—your attention. When you talk with her, it often helps to have real objects that she can handle, pictures of things that are familiar to her, and simple books with clear pictures that show lots of information. Children can learn another language with amazing speed and they generally learn best through lots of meaningful talk with those who speak the language they want to learn.

In this handbook, you'll find many options for helping English learners. Additionally, we explain some general principles about teaching a second language that are good to know:

- Talk a lot with your partner. And, whenever possible, use pictures, gestures, and concrete objects to make yourself understood. In other words, when you say "I am so hungry!" rub your stomach, lick your lips, and look longingly at the pictures of food you've cut out of magazines or newspaper grocery ads.

- When your partner responds to you with a single word or phrase, use that word or phrase in a complete sentence so that she learns how to express herself more completely. For example, when Maria says, "Pencil," pointing to a pencil that needs sharpening, you might say, "Your pencil needs to be sharpened. Let me show you how to sharpen your pencil."

- Choose books with simple, repetitive, natural language that will make sense to your partner and that she'll learn to use herself. These patterns include: "This is . . ."; "Here is . . ."; "I can . . ."; or, "I see. . . ."

- Read books to her that will introduce her to new words. Look for books that feature clear pictures with labels: "these are the foods we eat, the clothes we wear, the games we play," and so on.

- Look for inviting pictures and glue them on posters or in blank book pages. Label them with simple phrases or sentences: *A bowl of ice cream* or *Here is a bowl of ice cream.*

- Find the books your partner loves and read them to her again and again. In this way, you'll build her language and give her every opportunity to understand the books and develop her confidence. It also helps to read books with a repetitive refrain such as "This is the house that Jack built."

- Discover as much as you can about your partner's first language and culture. The more you understand, the more effective you can be. You might even try to learn a few words of her home language.

- Most of all, remember to value what your partner knows. (She knows a lot, even if she can't express herself easily in her new language.) Build on that base.

Imagine learning a second language while you are learning to read and write. This is a big challenge. Your individual attention and support will make a big difference.

TAKE NOTE

So how can you tell if your partner is really learning? There's one sure and simple way to know. Watch her! You can determine from watching what she does and what she says whether she is learning and enjoying her time with you. You may want to jot some personal notes in a notebook so you can keep track of the learning you do with your partner. You can also revisit your notebook from time to time and think about how your tutoring work is progressing. What's working? What's not working as well? What changes might you make?

Notice what your partner is doing as you ask yourself:

◆ Does my partner like to talk with me?

◆ What does she notice and talk about when I read books to her? The pictures? The print? Letter sounds?

◆ Does she pretend to read a book she knows well? Is she beginning to read a few familiar words or lines?

◆ How does my partner respond when I write her name or the name of a family member? Does she try to write it? Can she find the first letter?

◆ What does my partner say about the pictures she's drawn or the marks that she makes for "writing"? Does she write any real letters (especially those from her name)?

◆ Is she thinking of messages and writing them in a way that looks like real writing? Is she learning a few words that she knows how to write?

If you work with an English learner, ask yourself:

◆ Can I correctly pronounce her name? (Don't hesitate to ask for help—and don't forget to practice!)

◆ Does she respond to me and seem to listen? Is she learning more words in English?

◆ Have I learned a few things to say in her language?

◆ Does she have favorite books, written in English, that she wants to hear again?

CHAPTER THREE

Can We Talk?

Talk with children! It's easy, fun, and one of the best ways to help. In our busy world, many children seldom have the opportunity to enjoy a real conversation with an adult. You have the golden opportunity to give one child your undivided attention every time you meet. In one year, talking for thirty minutes twice a week equals thirty-six hours of conversation! Of course, you and your partner will do more than just talk. You will read and write. But as children learn more about language—what it is and how to use it—they become stronger readers and writers.

FINDING WAYS TO TALK WITH CHILDREN

Sometimes it's difficult to begin talking with a young child you don't know. This section offers some ways to make it easier.

Getting to know the child

Talk to the teacher and find out as much as you can about your young partner's interests. Ask,

- What does he do well?

- What kinds of books does he seem to enjoy or ask for?

- Does he have a favorite author or illustrator?

- What does he do with his friends?

- What kinds of things does he share about his family?

- Does he have pets? A teddy bear? A favorite family member, such as a grandmother?

- What subjects interest my partner in the classroom?

- Is there any special information I should know (for example, can he play the piano or has he moved recently)?

The more you know about your partner, the easier it will be to choose good books for him—books that will match his interests. For instance, if your partner talks about his pet cat, you might look for a book about cats you know he'll enjoy. In the same way, knowing your partner well will help you help him write. If he is having trouble thinking of something to write about, you can step in and suggest a topic that you know he knows something about.

Opening a conversation

Watch your partner and watch the classroom to see how things work. In this way, you'll learn even more about your partner—information that you can use for conversation. Generally, it is better to begin a conversation with a child with comments rather than questions. For example, Daren was drawing a picture of himself and his friend riding bikes. Michael, a volunteer from a university program, said, "I like to ride my bike, too. I have a racer." That was the perfect entry into a lively conversation about bikes.

Talking about books

When you and your partner have something to focus on together, such as a book you are reading, the conversation often flows. You can talk about the pictures or the characters in the book. And here are some additional topics for conversation that you might try while you are reading a book to your partner:

Discussing how the story is like something in the child's life or yours	"That's like . . . " "That reminds me of . . . "
Noting a favorite or funny part	"That was funny, wasn't it, when . . . " "I liked the part when . . . " "What part did you like best?"
Inviting the child to notice the details of the pictures	"Look at . . ." "What do you see in the picture?"
Pointing out the people or animals in the book and what they are like	"That [person or animal] is funny, isn't he?" "What do you think [the character] is going to do?"

"What would you do?

"What do you think [the character] is thinking?"

Wondering what might happen next

"What do you think is going to happen?"

"I think [event] might happen."

You can ask questions that invite the child to comment, but good conversation is a give-and-take adventure. Instead of asking lots of questions, share some of your own opinions and experiences. In this way, you'll encourage your partner to share his ideas. A good book conversation will sound like two friends enjoying a book together. Both ask questions. Both laugh at something in the book or predict what might happen next. Both notice and comment on interesting details in the pictures.

Talking while writing

Before your partner begins writing, talk with him about what he wants to say. After you've chatted for a while, you can ask, "What could you write about that?" Once he starts writing, help him think about what he wants to say next. It isn't easy to think of what to write or how to express it, but the more experience the child has, the easier it will be for him. He will write best about what he's interested in and what is meaningful to him. And as you talk with him, you learn what interests him.

EXPANDING CHILDREN'S TALK

No matter how we talk, we want our friends to listen and respond thoughtfully to what we say. As volunteers it is not our role to correct children's speech. In fact, correcting someone's speech does not necessarily produce the desired effect. It may even destroy the trust required for a successful relationship. You can help children develop their language just by listening and talking about topics that are of interest to them.

What should you do if a child uses "incorrect grammar"? Simply respond in a natural way:

CHILD: I goed home late."

ADULT: "Oh, you went home late. Why were you late?"

The child shows that he knows how to form the past tense by adding *ed*, but he has overgeneralized this form to the irregular *go*. Children are able to hear language that is different from their own and will gradually learn to talk in a way that sounds standard and conventional. They don't need to be told that what they are saying is "bad" or "incorrect." The surest way to silence children is to correct them frequently.

TAKE NOTE

From time to time, think about your conversations with your partner:

◆ Does my partner initiate conversations with me instead of waiting for me to talk first?

◆ Is our conversation easy, like that of one friend to another?

◆ Is my partner growing and changing in the language he uses?

◆ Is my partner talking for a longer duration, using some of the language I use, and using language from books?

◆ Is my partner using language in many ways; for example, asking questions, telling stories, or reporting information?

*Expanding
Children's Talk*

CHAPTER **FOUR**

Get Lost in a Book

The magic of language and books comes to life when we read aloud to children. Indeed, no instructional method we might choose can equal the power and joy of simply reading aloud a good book. When you read to children on a regular basis, you add immeasurably to the language resources of the classroom. In this chapter we share some of the ways that reading aloud can carry children into literacy.

THE VALUE OF READING ALOUD TO CHILDREN

Many of us remember with great fondness our own bedtime stories and the joy of commanding an adult's full attention during story time. Reading aloud benefits all children in all ways, but it is especially important for those children who aren't read to at home. Such is the reality for many children today as their adult family members must often struggle to earn a living, leaving little time, if any, for the pleasure of reading.

While the benefits of reading aloud are many, we have organized them into three categories: enjoyment, expanding knowledge, and skills.

The joy of reading

When you read to a child, you:

- Show that you enjoy reading books and demonstrate that reading can be magical and great fun.

- Invite the child to have fun while listening to a story.

- Invite the child to join in on parts of the book that showcase enjoyable language, such as a rhythmical, repeating refrain.

- Create interest in other books.

Knowledge

When you read to a child, you:

- Expand a child's knowledge of the world, introducing her to information, concepts, and realities she has not seen or experienced.

- Help the child learn sets of knowledge such as colors, days of the week, and the four seasons.

- Add to the words that the child knows and can use in other ways.

- Introduce the child to authors and artists who write and illustrate books.

- Build the child's storehouse of literacy and literary experiences.

Skills

When you read to a child, you:

- Expose her to the unique ways written language sounds.

- Build her awareness of the sounds of words (phonics).

- Enable the child to notice relationships between the way words sound and the letters on the page (phonics).

- Demonstrate smooth, phrased reading.

- Prompt the child to notice all the ways print works, such as moving in a specific direction, left to right and top to bottom.

- Help the child discover how books are put together, with a beginning, a middle, and an end.

- Help the child notice how a reader turns pages, moves through the book, and keeps the focus on an enjoyable story.

GETTING READY TO READ ALOUD

Select a book for a child or a small group and get ready to read.

Previewing the book

Preview the book by reading and thinking about it on your own. Consider:

- What ideas in the book could you link to children's lives (such as a new baby brother or a pet)?

- Can you link the book to any other books you have read to the children?

- What concepts or ideas in the book might be new to children?

- What words or language patterns might be unfamiliar?

- What parts of the book might be especially interesting to the children?

- Are there places in the story where you can stop and invite the children to predict what will happen next?

- What conversations might you have about the book's illustrations? How do the illustrations add to the story?

If possible, anticipate new knowledge and words the children might not know. Be prepared to talk with them to help them understand the book. You can even write notes to yourself on Post-its and mark the pages you want to discuss.

Finding a location

Find a relatively quiet area where you can read to your partner or to several children without being interrupted. Be sure that you and your partners are comfortable and that they can see the book and hear you. If you are working in a school classroom, find an out-of-the-way area, such as a corner where your group is protected from classroom traffic patterns.

HOLDING AND LOOKING AT THE BOOK

Most of the time, you will be reading to one child at a time; however, there might be times when there are two or three students clustered around you. We will discuss holding and looking at the book in both situations.

Reading to one child

The great value of reading aloud to one child is that you can then give her your undivided attention. The two of you sit close together, side by side, so that she can see and touch the pictures. Here are some suggestions:

- Hold the book so she can see the print and pictures while you read.

- Read in a clear, expressive voice, changing your voice to represent the story characters' dialogue.

- Be careful not to obscure the print or pictures with your hand.

- Observe the child's interest in the pictures and invite her to explore and touch them.

Reading to several children

You will probably not read to the entire class, but you may read to a small group. If possible, we recommend that you limit the group to three or four

Figure 4–1 *Volunteer Reading to Two Children*

children. The suggestions we have just outlined also apply when you are reading with more than one child. Make sure that all children can see the pictures and hear you read. Some readers hold the book up and off to one side, facing it forward so everyone in the group can see. If you have only two listeners, however, one can sit on either side of you and see and touch the pictures while you read (Figure 4–1).

With the teacher's help, make it clear to the children who are not in your group that you cannot be interrupted while you are reading. Small interruptions to answer other children's questions, help with work, sharpen pencils, or get supplies will make the reading ineffective. If other children approach you, tell them firmly that you are reading.

TALKING ABOUT THE BOOK

In Chapter 3 we discussed the value of conversation. Without disrupting your reading momentum too much, talk with your reading partners about the book you are reading. In other words, reading aloud doesn't mean that the adult reads while the children are silent. You and your reading partners will talk about the story in different ways. Next, we share several opportunities that might lead to conversation.

Asking what the book is about

The book begins with a cover. Sometimes when adults read to children, they skip right to the beginning of the story. But there's so much to learn from looking at the whole book first. After all, that's what readers do. When they pick up a book, they examine it closely. They want to discover what it's about, and they want to know something about the author who wrote it.

Talk with the children about the book cover. What do we find on the cover? Help the child locate the book title and the author's and illustrator's names. Often a picture or design suggests what the book is about. Many books have a large cover picture that you can see when you open the book and lay it flat, looking at the front and back cover together. Explaining these features of the book will help your young partners become literate individuals who understand how books work.

On the inside of the cover are the "endpapers," which often feature colors and beautiful designs or artwork. These designs are carefully planned to enhance the reader's experience.

An author may also write a short note dedicating the book to someone special. The child often finds this information fascinating. We have found that when readers point out these features of authorship, children start using them in their own writing.

Talking about what you might find in the book before you begin reading helps children anticipate what they will encounter and enhances their comprehension of the story. You can also introduce the child to the book by connecting it to other books you've read together. And you can always connect a new book to something special you know about your partner.

Asking what the pictures say

We want children to learn how to use information from pictures. Talking with an adult volunteer can help the child notice details in a picture that will help her understand the story. Point out details to the child. Ask her to touch the pictures, noticing significant information that extends the story. Be prudent; you don't want to make this activity a "test," but you do want to demonstrate the way in which illustrations can tell a story, too.

For example, when reading *The Mitten* by Alvin Tresselt, a folktale in which many animals stuff themselves into a mitten until it bursts, a volunteer said, "Oh, look, that mitten's getting really full." The comment prompted the child to look closely at the picture, point to a loose thread, and say, "It's starting to break."

Balancing talk and reading

Talk is important, but it's also necessary to keep the story going so that the child can understand it. Stop for conversation, but not for so long or so often that you lose your reading momentum. Brief conversations enhance the child's understanding of the story and give her a chance to use the language she hears in the book.

If you find that your conversation about the book is slipping away from the book itself, you can say, "Let's find out what happens in the story now," or "Let's talk about that at the end of the story," or, simply begin reading again. You will recapture the child's attention right away.

Talking to understand

Talking about the story helps children understand what you are thinking about as you are reading the story. It helps them grasp what the whole story is about as well as learn unfamiliar ideas or words. Comments can also help children think about books in the way good readers do. For instance, readers often make predictions about a story as they are reading it. They:

- Wonder about characters or events in the story.

- React personally to the illustrations or to what happens to the characters.

- See the humor in a situation.

- Figure out what a character is like and what she might be doing next.

Talking after the story

After the story, give your reading partner a chance to respond briefly. Your conversation should sound like two friends talking about something they have experienced together. Don't turn it into a test and fire off question after question. Your thoughtful comments about the book will encourage your partner to offer similar thoughtful observations.

Try these techniques to help your partner think and talk:

- That story reminded me of . . .

- I like the way the author surprised me at the end.

- I'm still wondering about . . .

- I was glad that . . .

- That was funny when . . . , wasn't it?

- I wish the author . . .

- That character made me think of . . .

- I don't understand why . . .

REREADING BOOKS

When children hear the same story over and over, they acquire new language and a deeper understanding of the story. They also notice new details in the pictures as they see them again. It doesn't make sense to reread books that children don't love, but they'll want to hear their favorites again and again.

Although the adult reader may grow bored with the same story, young children seldom do. They enjoy the nuances of the well-loved language. They revel in reliving the story. And they make the book their own as they absorb the storybook language, plot structures, and character development. Hearing beloved stories repeatedly often helps children make an intuitive leap into literacy.

What books are good to reread? You might try:

- Favorites that children ask for over and over (such as Henkes' *Julius, the Baby of the World*, or Hill's *Where's Spot?*).

- Books with strong stories and enjoyable language (such as Marshall's *The Three Little Pigs* or Galdone's *Jack and the Beanstalk*).

- Books with memorable characters that children come to love (for example, Rey's *Curious George*, Brown's *Arthur's Tooth*, and Parish's *Amelia Bedelia*).

- Books that offer a chance to practice using sets of knowledge (such as an alphabet book, a counting book, a book about colors, or a book of zoo animals).

- Books with rhythm and rhyme that invite children to join in (such as Martin's *Chicka, Chicka, Boom, Boom* or Galdone's *Over in the Meadow*).

LISTING THE BOOKS YOU'VE READ

Here's an idea your partner will enjoy. Keep a small notebook that lists all the books you have read together. Add a brief comment about each book. This shows your partner that reading books is important. It helps you remember the fun you've had with books and gives you both a sense of accomplishment as your list grows.

At the end of each reading session, while your partner watches, add to the reading list or make another check by a book you've read many times. Your partner may help you write the list, perhaps adding a letter or two, a familiar word, or the entire title. Some children can copy the title easily; for others it may be too tedious. In that case, it's easier for you to share the writing with the child or do it for her. The list isn't about record keeping. It's a celebration! It's something you and the child create together to reinforce and celebrate your reading pleasure and accomplishments.

Figure 4–2 is an example of a record of read-aloud sessions.

Figure 4–2

BOOKS WE HAVE READ TOGETHER

Title	Author	Comment
Dear Willie Rudd	Gray	It makes me sad inside
Chrysanthemum	Henkes	Another funny book!
The Red Poppy	Light	The photographs are awesome
Aunt Flossie	Howard	Aunt Flossie is like my aunt.

TAKE NOTE

From time to time ask yourself some questions about what happens when you read with your partner:

◆ Is my partner involved, wanting to hear more stories or reread her old favorites?

◆ Does she initiate conversations about the cover, the illustrations, or the story?

◆ Does she join in on the stories I reread, make predictions about what might happen next, and talk about the story after reading?

◆ Does she notice similarities between the books I read to her or connect books to her own life experiences?

CHAPTER **FIVE**

Find Books to Love

"Read it again!" These three magic words tell you that the book you chose to read aloud to your young partner hit the mark. A successful read-aloud session begins with a good book, so choose carefully. Use these guidelines to find books your partner will love:

- Select books that you can read in one sitting (about fifteen minutes at the most). Otherwise, the child can lose the sense of story in between sittings.

- Read a variety of genres—poetry, folk tales, fairy tales, real world stories (for example, stories about children and their families), informational stories, and others.

- Read a book without words. It might seem strange, but wordless books offer exciting opportunities for children to talk about the pictures and to make up the story using the detailed information available in the pictures.

- Choose books that contribute to children's knowledge in important ways and relate to children's personal interests.

- Look for books that reflect a wide diversity of human experience. Our goal is to expand children's conceptual and emotional vistas, so look for books that include stories about people of color, people with different languages and cultures, and people who face different physical and mental challenges.

SOME GUIDELINES

When you visit the library or a bookstore, use these guidelines to find books children will love:

- Search for stories that children can relate to their own lives; for example, stories about friends, siblings, grandparents, pets, school.

> **Examples:**
>
> *Abuela* by Arthur Dorros
>
> *My Best Friend* by Pat Hutchins
>
> *Grandmother and I* by Helen Buckley
>
> *Mouse Views* by Bruce MacMillan
>
> *A Chair for My Mother* by Vera Williams
>
> *My Name is Marcia Isabel* by Ana M. Cerro

- Look for books that expand vocabulary; for example, books that feature clearly labeled illustrations (such as foods we eat, clothes we wear, or colors we know).

> **Examples:**
>
> *Red Is Best* by Kathy Stinson
>
> *Growing Colors* by Bruce MacMillan
>
> *Eating the Alphabet* by Lois Ehlert
>
> *My House, Mi Casa* by Rebecca Emberley

- Delight children with lively books that feature rhythm, rhyme, and repetition. They are such fun and a great way to discover the sounds and patterns of language.

> **Examples:**
>
> *Chicka, Chicka, Boom, Boom* by Bill Martin
>
> *Three Billy Goats Gruff* by Paul Galdone
>
> *Pumpkin, Pumpkin* by Jeanne Titherington
>
> *Time for Bed* by Mem Fox

- Investigate books that help children develop "knowledge sets" such as the alphabet, days of the week, number words, color words, months, animals, clothing, and so forth.

> **Examples:**
>
> *Twenty-Six Letters and Ninety-Nine Cents* by Tana Hoban
>
> *A Big Fat Hen* by Keith Baker
>
> *The Very Hungry Caterpillar* by Eric Carle
>
> *Who Said Red* by Mary Serfozo
>
> *How Many Bugs in a Box?* by David Carter

- Surround children with the many pleasures of poetry.

> **Examples:**
>
> *Mary Had a Little Lamb* by Sara Josepha Hale
>
> *Sing a Song of Popcorn* by Beatrice de Regniers
>
> *Tomie de Paola's Mother Goose* by Tomie de Paola

- Expand children's knowledge of the world by offering them experiences that they might otherwise miss.

> **Examples:**
>
> *At the Crossroads* by Rachel Isadora
>
> *Koko's Kitten* by Francine Patterson
>
> *Tar Beach* by Faith Ringgold

- Introduce children to informational books.

> **Examples:**
>
> *The Cloud Book* by Tomie de Paola
>
> *Trucks* by Byron Barton
>
> *The Chef* by Douglas Florian

- Engage children with the classics.

Examples:

Goldilocks and the Three Bears (a good version by Paul Galdone and another by James Marshall)

Lon Po Po: A Red Riding Hood Story From China by Ed Young

Korean Cinderella by Shirley Climo

■ Intrigue children with several versions of the same story. They read each version and discover how the same story can be told in slightly different ways but retain its classic components with the same basic plot and characters. You can also turn the story around and tell it from the viewpoint of a different character. Children find an exploration of alternative viewpoints great fun, and it deepens their understanding of the nature of stories.

Examples:

The Three Little Pigs by Paul Galdone

The Three Little Pigs by James Marshall

The True Story of the Three Little Pigs by Jon Scieszka

The Three Little Pigs and the Fox by William Hooks

The Three Little Wolves and the Big Bad Pig by Eugene Trivizas and Helen Oxenbury

■ Read several favorites by the same author. Children will come to view the author as a friend.

Some Favorite Authors for Young Children Are:[1]

Alma Flor Ada	Eric Hill
Jan Brett	Pat Hutchins
Marc Brown	Ezra Jack Keats
Eric Carle	Bill Martin
Donald Crews	Bruce MacMillan
Lois Ehlert	Patricia Polacco

[1]At least one book by each author is included in the booklist at the end of this handbook.

Paul Galdone	Cynthia Rylant
Carmen Lomes Garza	Vera Williams
Gail Gibbons	Audrey Wood
Kevin Henkes	

- Explore series of books that feature the same character in book after book.

Examples:[2]

Arthur	*Henry and Mudge*
Amelia Bedelia	*Little Bear*
Amazing Grace	*Nate the Great*
Curious George	*Madeleine*
Clifford the Big Red Dog	*Mr. Putter & Tabby*
Frog and Toad	*Spot*
	Cam Jansen

- Search for wordless picture books—they are always a hit with young children.

Examples:

Pancakes for Breakfast by Tomie de Paola

Good Dog Carl (series) by Alexandra Day

Deep in the Forest by Brinton Turkle

BOOKS TO READ ALOUD

There are many ways to get the books that you need to read to children:

- The classroom teacher may ask you to read particular books to your young partner.

- The child may make a special request for an author or topic that she likes.

- The school librarian may be helpful in choosing books that children like.

[2]Books about these characters may be found in the booklist at the end of this handbook. Look for the name of the character in the book titles.

- You may ask your friends to donate no-longer-needed books from their own children's collections.

- You may find all of the books listed in this handbook in bookstores and public libraries.

- You may want to check the reference books in libraries that list books on particular topics.

Consider getting a basket or small plastic tub to store books that are good to read aloud. You may be able to keep this container in a special place in the classroom or a work room so it's always available. If you have access to many good books to read aloud, you can organize them by category in several tubs or baskets.

TAKE NOTE

At the end of this guide you'll find lists of books that are "Too Good to Miss" (Appendix A). We have listed thirty books for each grade level—kindergarten, first, second, and third. Use the list in a flexible way. After all, a quality book works at any grade level.

Keep in mind the guidelines in this chapter and you'll know how to choose the best books for your reading partner. As you think about your selection of books, you may find the following questions helpful:

- ◆ Do I have a variety of books with different characters and stories that reflect a rich diversity of people?

- ◆ Do I have some of the "classic" stories and multiple versions of the same stories?

- ◆ Do I have books that will enhance children's knowledge, vocabulary, and skill?

- ◆ Do *I* like all of the books I am reading to children?

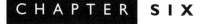

CHAPTER SIX

Discover Shared Reading

Our ultimate goal, of course, is to help children become independent readers who know their way around books and who look for every opportunity to escape inside them. Yes, we want children to get lost—routinely—in good books! Shared reading is a way to help young readers grow from listening to stories to reading stories themselves. Shared reading supports children as it involves them more actively in reading.

In shared reading, children read the same book at the same time in unison with the adult. You might think of two people singing a song together or reading responses together in church. The less experienced reader—the child—is supported by the adult so that she can take an active role in the reading and behave like an accomplished reader.

THE VALUES OF SHARED READING

The values of shared reading are many. Let's list some of the advantages. Children:

- Learn what smooth, fluent reading sounds like and feels like.

- Follow print first with their fingers and eyes. Later, they learn to use their eyes alone.

- Learn how print works—that it moves left to right and that they must match one spoken word to one printed word.

- Revisit what they know about print. Again and again, they can spot words, letters, and punctuation marks they know.

- Learn how sentences are laid out on the page.

- Figure out new words by examining the sounds related to the first letter of the word as well as the middle and final letters.

- Say and see the words that will build their beginning reading vocabulary. These are words that they recognize quickly and easily as they read other materials.

Finding books to read

Shared reading requires special attention to the reading materials because the child must be able to see the lines of print. For example:

- The print must be clear and easy to read.

- The material must be simple, with only a few lines of print on each page and some repeating patterns—something your partner can soon read herself.

- The material may be a rhyme or poem that your partner will enjoy reading over and over.

- The material may be books or stories that your partner has read before or a text that's brand new.

- The material must be something that you both enjoy because you will read it over and over.

In some classrooms, teachers may use oversized books with very large print. Known as "big books," these work well for shared reading with the whole class or a small group. You do not need big books when you are working with one or two children. In fact, if you and the children are trying to use a big book, you will find that the print is too large and the book is hard to handle. We recommend regular books.

> **Recommended Books for Shared Reading:**
>
> *The Chick and the Duckling* by Mirra Ginsburg
>
> *Where's Spot?* by Eric Hill
>
> *Shoes for Grandpa* by Mem Fox
>
> *The Napping House* by Audrey Wood
>
> *Goodnight Owl* by Pat Hutchins
>
> *King Bidgood's in the Bathtub* by Audrey Wood
>
> *We're Going on a Bear Hunt* by Helen Oxenbury

Figure 6–1 *Shared Reading Poem*

Mary Had a Little Lamb

Mary had a little lamb—
its fleece was white as snow.
Everywhere that Mary went
the lamb was sure to go.

Sometimes, when few materials are available, teachers write poems or rhymes in large print on blank paper and use them over and over for shared reading with children. Posters and charts work well, too. In Figure 6–1, you see how one literacy volunteer wrote a poem on a large sheet of cardboard.

The following list showcases examples of simple familiar songs and rhymes excellent for shared reading.

Songs:

Happy Birthday to You

Itsy, Bitsy Spider

Nursery Rhymes:

Mary Had a Little Lamb

Jack and Jill

Humpty Dumpty

Counting Rhymes:

This Little Piggy Went to Market

One, Two, Buckle My Shoe

One Potato, Two Potato

SHARING READING TOGETHER

Sharing the reading task supports children who are just learning to read, but it also helps older children learn to read more fluently. When you read books with early readers, you point frequently to the words while reading or slide a pointer underneath the words. With more experienced readers who no longer need to point to each word, the adult and child simply follow the print with their eyes and read together.

Shared reading means reading together. *Be sure that all the readers can see the print clearly*. You might sit side by side with printed material on a desk or table, but you can also post printed material on an easel or on the wall. If the material is on the wall, you might find that a slim, short pointer (like an unsharpened pencil or a chopstick) helps your partner focus attention on each word as it is read. Point to the words from the very beginning, even with an early reader. *Be sure to point under the words rather than on top of them.* We recommend crisply pointing to each word rather than sweeping under the line of print. The idea is to notice the individual words. Use the pointer yourself, demonstrating how to point under each word and read. Gradually, with experience, the child can take a turn using the pointer.

If the story or poem is new to the child, read it to her as many times as needed before she begins to join in on the reading with you. Enjoy it together, moving gradually toward sharing the reading. If the child has read the story many times, you can read all the pages together.

Often books have difficult and easy parts. You read the harder parts and let the child join in or read alone the easier parts. For example, in a shared reading of Mirra Ginsburg's *The Chick and the Duckling*, the text has a description of what the duckling does. The chick copies the duckling, each time saying, "Me, too." Children enjoy hearing an adult read the descriptions of action and then find it easy to read, "Me, too." The print in this book is large and easy to see. The pictures support the child's understanding of the story events.

An advantage of shared reading is that you and your reading partner progress right through the book, turning pages and moving along the lines of print with enthusiasm and expression. In this way, the child gets the feel of being a reader. You won't have many opportunities to stop for conversation because talk would interrupt your reading, but you and your partner can talk about the reading afterward.

TAKE NOTE

After you and your partner have tried shared reading, ask yourself:

◆ Does my partner seem to enjoy shared reading?

◆ Is she able to read some or all of the book with me and point to the words while reading?

◆ Can my partner (once she becomes a more capable reader) follow the print with her eyes, keeping up with me as we read?

◆ Does she stop and notice when what she reads and says does not match the print on the page?

◆ Is my partner learning to read more and more of the text for herself, noticing and acquiring new words?

CHAPTER SEVEN

What It Takes to Read

W e can't learn without making mistakes. Think about anything you've learned. Chances are you made your share of missteps as you mastered your new skill. Learning to read is no different. Children will make mistakes. We lend them a hand, but we also need to let them stumble a bit as they work out the details of what reading is and how it works. As a volunteer, you offer the young reader support, but he does the work. He reads most of the book independently, working problems out for himself most of the time. In this way, he develops the problem-solving strategies he needs for skillful reading.

WHAT IS READING?

Reading is complex. Some researchers dedicate their professional careers to studying it. It is not the purpose of this handbook to cover the wide range of information about what reading is or how children learn to read. We include the information that will help you most in your work with children. And we offer this definition of reading as a helpful guide for your work:

> Readers gain the author's meaning when they connect what they
> know about the world and about language to printed words.

Let's consider what skillful readers do when they read. While we can't peek inside their heads, we can infer that they must be:

- Noticing the print forms and connecting them to meaningful words.

- Using sequences of sounds to figure out words.

- Using the print—clusters of letters or words—and connecting it with words that have meaning.

- Thinking about what the sentence or story might say and checking with the print to be sure they match.

- Noticing when things don't make sense, don't sound right, or don't look right (don't match with the letters, sounds, or print patterns).

- Using knowledge about the direction in which the eyes should move.

- Reading mostly correctly while keeping the meaning in mind.

- Reading fluently and putting words together in phrases when they read out loud.

- Doing all of this with great speed, largely without thinking about it.

Beginning readers, of course, cannot perform with such speed and accuracy. At first, when children are just learning to read, the process may seem tedious. That's because they are trying all at once to put all of the pieces of the reading process together into one meaningful whole.

The more successful reading experiences young children have, the easier learning to read becomes. That's why the books you select for your reading partner should offer some challenge but, in general, be fairly easy for the child to read. Struggling to read a book does not help children learn to read fluently. They may come to view reading as a painful experience they'd rather avoid. Fast, pleasurable, easy reading, on the other hand, builds skills every time children read.

WORKING WITH BEGINNING READERS

What do we mean by the term "beginning readers"? Typically, these are kindergartners or first graders, although some will be second and third graders. They are just becoming familiar with print and are reading their first little books. The following sections offer some suggestions for supporting beginning readers.

In the beginning

We once believed that children had to know all their letters and many words before they could begin to read real books. We now know that children can begin to read simple little books while they continue to learn more about letters and words. The key is to start with books that will be easy for the reader. What is an easy book? Let's examine *Look at Me*[1] (Figure 7–1). *Look at Me* is designed to be easy for a beginning reader because it:

[1]*Look at Me* is a KEEP BOOK™ published by The Ohio State University Early Literacy Learning Initiative. It was written by Irene C. Fountas and illustrated by Sue Simon. See Chapter 11 for more information.

Figure 7–1 Look at Me *Text*

- Features one line of print on a page so the reader does not have to return to the beginning of the second line to read.

- Uses words that appear frequently in oral and written language; these words include *I*, *me*, *have*, and *at*.

- Features material that is familiar to most young children.

- Includes pictures that reveal clues to the written message.

- Uses repeating, often rhythmical, language patterns.

- Uses complete sentences so that children learn about the grammatical structure of written language.

Books like *Look at Me* offer a very easy task for the beginning reader. As the child reads and rereads *Look at Me* and other easy books, he will become more familiar with words that appear frequently in language and print, such as *I* and *have*, and will use word and letter knowledge as part of reading. This process is not the same as memorizing a book. Of course, the simple story is easy to remember, but what the young reader is actually doing is:

- Thinking about the story and remembering some of the language.

- Using the print to read and get the message.

- Recognizing some words and features of words.

- Using the pictures as additional information.

- Checking on his reading in many different ways.

Please point!

When you are working with a beginner, encourage the child to point to words while reading. The print in *Look at Me* is carefully positioned so that children can successfully use the "black marks and white spaces." Children who are matching well are "reading the spaces," matching their spoken words to the clusters of letters. They look for large word units and word breaks. In this way, they connect sounds with letters.

The hand can help the eyes in this early attempt to match spoken words with the print on the page. In books like *Look at Me*, the young reader can use his finger to point to each word, building the sense of motion he needs. Later, his eyes will take over.

Which way does the print go?

We read print from left to right. Children need to learn to move left to right across the printed words and then to sweep back to the left again to begin the next line. Sometimes this movement is difficult. That's why starting young children on books with one line of print per page is so important.

In the book *Watch Me!*[2] (Figure 7–2) the child is required to sustain

---

[2]*Watch Me!* is a KEEP BOOK written by Tina Henry and published by The Ohio State University Early Literacy Learning Initiative.

Figure 7–2 Watch Me! *Text*

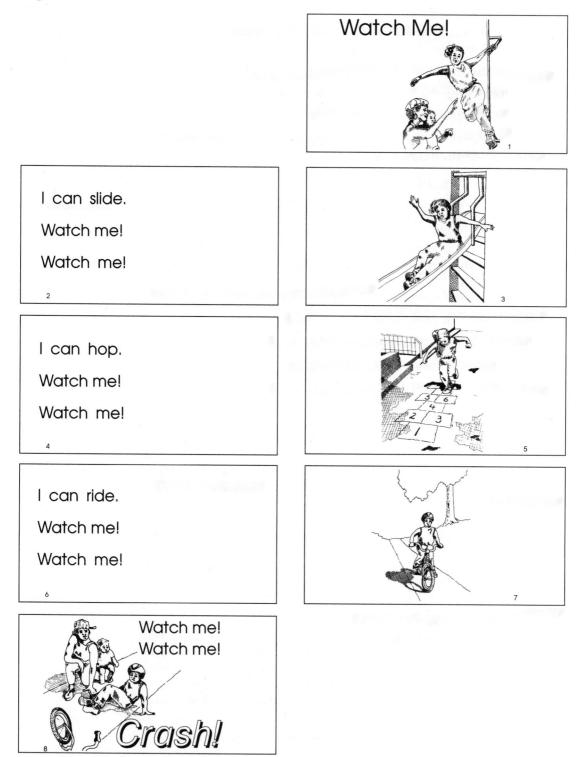

coordinated movement of his finger and eyes over three lines of text. *Watch Me!* is an easy book, but it is just a little harder to read than *Look At Me*.

The first word in *Watch Me!*, *I*, is very easy. Many children learn that word right away even if they do not yet fully understand the difference between a word and a letter. The first word of a line is hard for children because they cannot get a clue from the pictures. They must look at the letters and figure it out. By beginning with *I* and moving to another easy and also predictable (if you know the story) word, *can*, this book helps the young reader get started. This is not memorization. Young readers know the meaning and language and find their cues in the print.

HELPING CHILDREN GROW AS READERS

If you are able to work with the same children over time, you will notice that many of them make rapid progress in learning to read. Sometimes, they seem to grow daily. First-grade children, for example, typically move from the early learning described above to reading long and complex books (in which they have to sound out and analyze many new words) in one school year.

Helping children become problem solvers

Although it's logical to think that reading every word correctly is good and making mistakes is bad, the process of reading is more complicated. When a child makes errors, he has the opportunity to learn how to work out words the way good readers do. It is this process of "working them out" that helps the child learn how to read for himself. When a child reads most of the words correctly and makes only a few errors, the book is "just right" for him to learn to read better.

A child who notices the mismatch between his own attempt at a word and the print on the page is checking on his own reading. He may look again at the word or consider what it's likely to be. He may correct the error himself or he may not. What counts is that the child is working as a problem solver who is noticing and using information.

If you immediately correct a child, telling him the word before he tries to figure it out, he will miss the opportunity to solve problems successfully himself and he may become a dependent reader. It's easy to determine if your partner is becoming a dependent reader. You'll find that he won't even attempt to read an unknown word but, instead, will appeal to you for help, look at you for some signal, or simply stop and wait.

Your goal as a literacy volunteer is to support and create active readers who keep trying and who know how to work on unknown words in a variety of ways. Instead of correcting or giving children the words when you listen to them read, use the three very helpful questions in Figure 7–3. Children can use these questions to check if they are right. These questions prompt children to use different sources of information.

Figure 7–3

QUESTIONS THAT HELP CHILDREN USE INFORMATION WHEN THEY READ	
When the adult asks	The child is prompted to consider whether or not what he reads fits with the
• Does that make sense?	• Story or the meaning (also pictures).
• Does that sound right?	• Way we talk.
• Does that look right?	• Way the word looks—letters and letter clusters and their relationship to sounds.

The chart in Figure 7–4 lists questions that help children solve problems they may encounter while reading. Consider clipping it to a clipboard or taping it on your notebook so that you can refer to it as you help children read. All of the actions and comments in the chart are helpful only when the child is reading a book that is just right for him. You will know when the book is too hard because he will struggle. If that happens, say, "Let's read this book together!" or, "I'll read this part," and then offer him another easier book.

Helping children learn to read fluently

Good readers not only read quickly, they also sound smooth and fluent; that is, they put their words together in phrases that sound very much like talking. To help children read more fluently:

- Give them easy books to read so that they do not have to stop so much.

- Demonstrate fluent reading by reading to them and doing lots of shared reading.

- For a book that the child is reading himself, read a small section demonstrating how you put words together in phrases and read smoothly. Then say, "Read it like I did."

- Comment and praise when children read with phrasing and expression.

- Point out the punctuation. Read to demonstrate how to pause at commas, how the voice goes up for a question, or down at the end of a sentence with a period.

- Say, "Try that again and put your words together."

- Ask (after reading), "Did that sound choppy or smooth?" Demonstrate if the child does not understand the question.

Helping children understand what is read

Remember our definition of reading. Reading means making sense of a text. If you don't understand what you are reading, you aren't really reading.

Figure 7–4

HELPING THE CHILD AT POINTS OF DIFFICULTY

What you can do when the child has difficulty:	Some examples of what you might say:
Give the child some time to notice the error and work things out. Wait, saying nothing.	[Afterward] "I like the way you worked that out."
Encourage him to try if he just stops.	"Try it." [Then praise the effort.]
Encourage the child to reread as a way of thinking of what the word could be.	"Go back and read that again. Think of what would make sense (or sound right)."
Encourage the child to reread the sentence up to the word and make the sound of the first letter. Demonstrate for the child how to do this.	"Go back, read that again, and start the word."
Praise the child's effort at problem solving even if he does not get the word right.	"You were really working hard." "I like the way you tried to work that out."
Pay attention and praise when the child notices and fixes errors for himself.	"Good checking!" "I like the way you noticed that and fixed it yourself."
Show that you value partially correct responses (when a child has made a good attempt but has not completely solved the word).	"You're nearly right. Try that again." "You've almost got that." [Point out a part that will help the child.]
Help the child to sound out word parts and then check to make sure they make sense in the story.	"Look at the beginning of the word. Now say more of the word." [You might guide the child's eyes to move along the word.] [After analyzing the word] "Would that make sense?"
Encourage the child to use what he knows about words.	"Do you know something about that word?" "Do you know a word like that?" "What do you know that can help?"
Stop the reading if the child is struggling on just about every word (the text is too hard). The child can read with you or you can read it to him.	"Let's read that together." Or, "I'll read the rest to you."

Many poor readers can pick their way through a text, sounding out words or saying words, but afterward they can't tell you what they read. Those readers generally read slowly and sound very choppy. Fluent reading, as we just described, is evidence that readers are putting words together in a way that shows they understand the book.

When you read with your partner, be sure he understands what he is reading. How can you assess his understanding? Talk briefly about the book before he tries to read it. Introduce him to the book's subject matter (what it's about) and some of the language that may be new to him. Look through the pictures together. Invite him to comment or ask questions. As he reads, you can stop periodically to chat about the reading ("Why do you think that happened?"). After he finishes reading, you'll want to discuss the whole book ("What did you think of the story?"). You can also encourage him to draw pictures about the story or write a response to it.

CHOOSING THE RIGHT BOOK

If you are in a situation where you are helping your partner read a book that he has not seen before, choose a book that you think will not be too hard for him. As a general rule of thumb, if the child struggles on every page, the book is too hard.

It is helpful to organize books from easy to harder in "leveled" sets. The first set, for example, includes the first ones you use with a beginner (like *Watch Me!*). The next set is just a little harder, and so on. We present a list of leveled books arranged from easier to harder in our book *Guided Reading* (1996). Your local library or school may have a reference copy.

TAKE NOTE

As you think about the ways in which you are helping your young partner learn to read, ask yourself these questions:

◆ Is my partner enjoying the reading I am doing with him?

◆ Is his reading smooth and phrased, and are the books easy enough for him so that he can correct his own errors?

◆ Is my partner getting better at figuring out new words while reading, always trying on his own before he asks for help?

◆ Is my partner learning to use a range of information to support his reading?

◆ Is he becoming a more skillful reader, able to read harder books?

◆ Does he talk about his reading in a way that lets me know he understands it?

The Place for Phonics, Letters, and Words

Good readers are able to use letter-sound relationships to figure out new words when they read. Teaching children about these relationships is usually called "phonics." Since the English language is an alphabetic system, learning about the sounds of the language and the symbols they represent is critical; however, children need to know more than simple letter-sound relationships. They need to know that words have patterns—clusters of letters that may be related to sounds.

UNDERSTANDING PHONICS

A particular professional vocabulary is generally associated with phonics instruction. Teachers use this vocabulary when they talk to each other about phonics, and sometimes they use the vocabulary with children. Figure 8–1 explores the vocabulary associated with phonics that may be helpful for you to know.

HELPING CHILDREN LEARN THE LETTERS OF THE ALPHABET

Children have a lot to learn about the letters of the alphabet. They need to learn the names of the letters, the sounds they match, and the most effec-

Figure 8–1

> ## VOCABULARY ASSOCIATED WITH PHONICS
>
> **consonants** (all the letters except *a, e, i, o,* and *u*)
>
> **vowels** (*a, e, i, o,* and *u*)
>
> > short vowel (the vowel sound in *hat, pet, hit, on,* and *up*)
> >
> > long vowel (the name of the vowel is the sound it makes, such as in *ape, eat, ice, use,* and *over*)
>
> **blends or consonant clusters** (a combination of two or three consonant letters, such as the *st* in *stop* or the *str* in *stream*)
>
> **digraphs** (two letters that make one sound, such as the *ch* in *chair* or *chorus,* or the *sh* in *shoe,* or the *wh* in *when* and *which*)
>
> **prefixes** (a group of letters added to the beginning of a word to change the meaning, such as *unpack* or *rewind*)
>
> **inflectional endings** (a letter or group of letters added to the end of a word, such as *s, ing, est,* as in *walks, hoping,* and *brightest*)
>
> **suffixes** (a group of letters added to the end of a word, such as *ful* or *ness,* as in *thankful* or *happiness*)
>
> **plurals** (a word that means more than one, for example, *cars, candies,* or *wolves*)
>
> **upper- and lowercase letters/capital letters and small letters** (the different forms of letters; lowercase or small letters are *a, b, c,* etc.; uppercase or capital letters are *A, B, C,* etc., and are used for a particular reason, such as to indicate the beginning of a sentence or to identify a proper name: *I have a dog named Rex.*)
>
> **syllables** (a group of letters pronounced as a unit in a word, with each part containing the sound of a vowel, as in *car-ton* and *to-ma-to*)

tive way to write them. Children must also understand how they can recognize letters when they encounter them in individual words or in words within a story. Learning the names of the letters gives children a way to talk about them. It helps them remember the letters when they look at them or write them. The following section includes some ideas for helping children learn the letters of the alphabet.

Figure 8–2 *Personal Alphabet Book*

Making personal alphabet books

Make a personal alphabet book with your young partner like the one we show in Figure 8–2. One letter, upper- and lowercase, appears on each page. Help the child choose a picture that corresponds with the letter and glue it on the page. Your partner can cut pictures out of magazines or newspapers. It's best to sort the pictures by the letters of the alphabet (put all the "a" pictures in one pile, "b" pictures in another, and so forth). Then guide the child's selection by identifying and saying the name of the object illustrated in each picture.

For example, referring to the page shown in Figure 8–2, the adult said, "Here are some things that start with 'a.' Let's say them together." They named the objects (apple, ant, alligator, airplane) and the child chose the apple.

Each day, you and your partner read the pages that have pictures, saying the letter name (in uppercase form and in lowercase) and the name of the picture beginning with the letter: "*Aa, apple, Bb, bear, Cc, car,*" and so on. Your goal is to help your partner recognize and read all the pages with ease. You may want to stop using the book after she knows all the letter names and most of the letter sounds.

Reading alphabet books

Alphabet books can be great fun and there are hundreds from which to choose—everything from very basic to intriguing and complex. Choose ones you know your partner will enjoy and talk about how the author and illustrator use the alphabet to convey information. Alphabet books help the child to organize her thinking about the alphabet, to recognize letters, and to learn more about letter names and letter sounds. Be selective about ABC books. Choose simple ones for young children. There are some wonderful ABC books for older children that are organized by the alphabet, but these may be too sophisticated for younger children.

> **Recommended Alphabet Books for Young Children:**
>
> *A Is for Apple* by Lynn N. Grundy
>
> *Action Alphabet* by Shelley Rotner
>
> *Alpha Bugs* by David A. Carter
>
> *Black and White Rabbit's ABC* by Alan Baker
>
> *A Helpful Alphabet of Friendly Objects* by David Updike
>
> *I Spy in the Garden* by Richard Powell
>
> *I Spy on the Farm* by Richard Powell
>
> *Old Black Fly* by Jim Aylesworth
>
> *Tomorrow's Alphabet* by George Shannon
>
> *26 Letters and 99 Cents* by Tana Hoban

Writing letters to learn letters

As children write the letters, they attend to their distinctive features. The differences between letters are small, and the motor movement of writing highlights the differences.

There are often small variations from school to school in the alphabet forms they choose to use. You will want to check with the teacher and obtain your school's guidelines for teaching children to form the letters. We have included one sample form of handwriting (Figure 8–3). Whenever you write for or with children, try to print carefully with forms as simple as these so that the children can easily recognize the letters.

Show children how to form each letter by explaining the process out loud as you write it; for example, for *b* you might say, "pull down, up and over," or for *I* you might say, "tall stick, top, bottom." Invite children to follow your lead and explain out loud as they attempt to form a letter. If children need additional help writing the letters, involve them in some of the following learning activities for two or three minutes. Children can:

- Trace letters using stencils or plastic forms.

- Write letters on paper with colored markers, in sand on a cookie tray, with a thin wet paint brush on a chalkboard (dip the brush in water), on a Magnadoodle[1] or magic slate—anywhere the children can write.

- Use multiple colors to write over a large letter you've written in pencil and create a "rainbow letter."

[1]A Magnadoodle is a commerically produced writing/erase board that can be purchased at most toy stores.

Figure 8–3a *Letter Formation Chart: Lowercase or Small Letters*

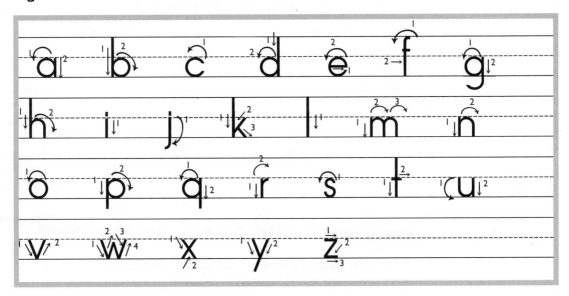

Figure 8–3b *Letter Formation Chart: Uppercase or Capital Letters*

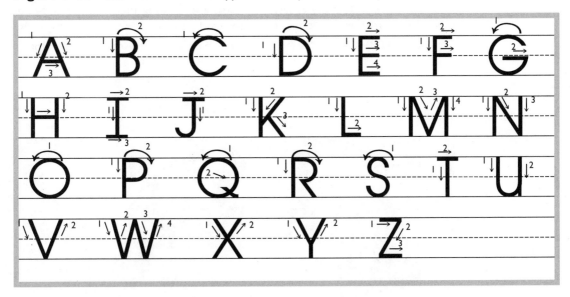

- Write letters on the chalkboard or on big sheets of chart paper making the letters large, middle sized, and small.

- Use thick or thin chalk on a board or try various colors of chalk.

Finding and sorting letters

Magnetic letters are brightly colored plastic letters with a magnet on the back. Word tiles are plastic squares with printed words on the front; they are often magnetic as well. You'll find them in many primary classrooms, and you can use them on most school chalkboards. They also work on some smaller chalkboards available in a toy store or school supply store. Before using a board with your partner, you might want to test its surface to see whether the small magnets on the back of alphabet letters will stick to it. A cookie sheet works quite well if no other surface is available.

Magnetic letters are especially helpful because the child can feel the letters and develop her ability to notice the distinctive features of each one. Place a group of magnetic letters on a flat surface—preferably a vertical one (Figure 8–4). Ask your partner to find a particular letter (such as the letters in her name). At first, you may not want to put out all twenty-six letters. Display four or five letters that the child knows and ask her to select from those. If many of the same letter are available, ask your partner to "find all the m's."

Magnetic letters are also good for sorting because they give children practice in looking at letter features and naming them. As the child sorts, ask her to say the letter name. You and your partner will enjoy exploring a variety of ways to sort letters:

Figure 8–4 *Letter Sort*

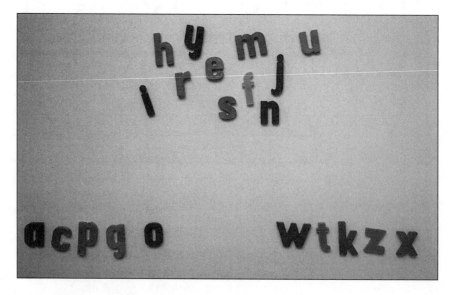

- Letters in my name and letters not in my name (*J a n e* and all the rest).

- Tall letters and short letters (*t, b, l, f* and *r, a, m, n*).

- Capital and lowercase letters (*T, M, L, S* and *t, m, l, s*).

- Capital and lowercase pairs (*Tt, Mm, Nn, Ss, Rr*).

- Letters with tails and letters with no tails (*g, y, p, q* and *a, r, s, t*).

- Letters with tunnels (*b, n, m, u*).

- Blue letters and red letters (for multicolored sets).

- Letters with circles and letters without circles (*a, b, d, g, p* and *r, j, t, s*).

- Letters in alphabetical order (*a, b, c, d, e*).

Making letter posters

Letter posters are always a hit with children and they are easy and inexpensive to make. An 11-by-17-inch sheet of poster board is just right. With a thick, dark marker, write the capital and lowercase letter at the top, bottom, or in the middle of the poster. Using magazines or newspapers, ask your partner to find things that begin with the letter and paste them all over the board. You might want to leave room to actually write the words under each picture. This activity is a good one to bridge home and school. Family members can help the child find pictures to bring to school. After she completes the poster, the child can take it home to keep.

WHAT'S IN A WORD?

Young children need to learn all sorts of information about words that may seem obvious to us as adult readers but that is brand new to them:

- Letters cluster together to make a word, and there is white space around words.

- A word is spelled the same whenever it appears—in different stories, in writing, on the board, etc.

- Words can be made up of one or more letters (*I, up, dog*).

- Words are sequences of sounds that are represented by letters and clusters of letters (*me, chair*).

- Words have parts that are like other words (*tree, try* or *day, play*).

- The sound of a word is a clue to the letters in it.

- Words can have letters that make no sounds (*make, lamb*).

- Words can be spelled the same and mean different things (*play, play*; *can, can*).

- Words can be spelled differently and sound the same (*to*, *too*, *two*).

- Words can be spelled the same but sound different depending on what is meant (*read*, *read*).

As children read and write, they learn what words are and how they work. Let's turn our attention now to focused word learning. There are several ways that you can help young children focus on words and learn more about them.

What's in a name?

All children love their own written names. Indeed, the most significant word a young child will ever learn is her name. So it comes as no surprise that children's written names are an excellent starting point for literacy learning. There are many ways to use children's names to help them begin reading and writing. Here are some suggestions:

- Show the child her written name on a card and ask her to copy it with magnetic letters.

- After she can write her first name, invite her to learn her last name, and then the names of her friends and family members.

- If you are in a classroom, ask your partner to look around the room and find her name.

- If you are not in a classroom, write the child's name on cards and place them around a room.

- Write the child's name in glue and sprinkle it with sand or glitter to make a word she can "feel."

- Make connections between the child's name and other words (for example, find words in a grocery advertisement that start like the child's name—*Madeleine*, *meat*, and *M&Ms*).

- Create a "name puzzle" (Figure 8–5). Write the child's name on strips of paper that are slightly elongated. Letter formation is important.

Figure 8–5 *Name Puzzle*

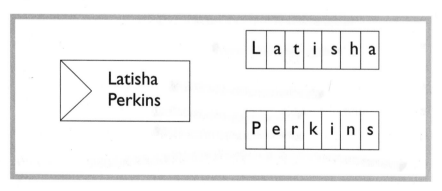

Then cut up the child's name, letter by letter, and place the individual letters in a manila envelope (or any other type of envelope) on which you've written her name. She can use the cut-up letters to reconstruct her name at school or at home. At first, she may need to look at the model of her name; later she can work without a model.

What's in a name? More than just the individual letters! As children participate in these activities and others, they learn much more than just how to read or write their names. They learn something about words and how they relate to other words. Through their own names, children discover how letters and sounds go together in words.

Helping children learn high-frequency words

Figure 8–6 is a list of about one-hundred words that appear often in our language. Known as "high-frequency" words, they occur again and again in the simple stories children read and in their own writing. It is helpful for them to "control" as many high-frequency words as possible. "Controlling high

Figure 8–6

HIGH-FREQUENCY WORDS				
a	day	if	old	this
after	did	in	on	three
all	do	into	one	to
an	don't	is	or	too
and	down	it	our	two
am	for	just	out	up
are	from	keep	over	us
as	get	kind	people	very
asked	go	know	play	was
at	going	like	put	we
away	good	little	ran	went
back	had	long	run	were
be	has	look	said	what
because	have	looked	saw	when
before	he	make	see	where
big	her	man	she	will
boy	here	me	so	with
but	him	mother	some	would
by	his	my	that	you
came	house	no	the	your
can	how	not	then	
come	I	now	there	
could	I'm	of	they	

frequency words" means that children can recognize them quickly and easily in reading and can write them quickly and easily in their own stories.

Recognizing some words quickly does not take the place of solving words by using letters and sounds. Children do need to know how to "sound out" word parts in reading. Every child needs the independence that comes from figuring out new words while reading. Nevertheless, children benefit from having a repertoire of words they recognize immediately and can use as examples to help them figure out new words.

When you notice your partner has difficulty reading or writing a particular word, make a note to yourself and then invite her to put the problem word together several times with magnetic letters. Here's what you can do to help your partner build her word knowledge:

- Make a list of high-frequency words your partner knows. Tape it on the wall or table, or put it in her writing folder or notebook so she can refer to it easily. She can use this list as a spelling check when she is writing.

- When you are doing shared reading or reading together (described in Chapter 7), ask the child to find some of these words.

- For children who have difficulty learning words, put the words on cards and place them in a box or on a ring holder. Review the words frequently, making a game of it. Encourage your partner to spend a few additional minutes learning one or two of the words that she found especially difficult. She can make them with magnetic letters or write them several times.

- Play card games with the words, such as "Concentration," "Go Fish," or other matching games.

- Show the child how to sort words (by first letter, last letter, or some other feature).

Noticing sounds and patterns in words

As they work with their teacher, children learn many skills related to taking words apart while reading and making words. If you are working in a classroom, ask the teacher about her priorities for word learning. To support children's awareness of sounds in words, write or use magnetic letters to build words that follow particular phonics principles (Figure 8–7). Create words:

- With silent letters (silent *e—like, make, bike, tape, rope*).

- That start alike (*box, bear, banana; store, stop, stamp*).

- That end the same (*hat, cat, must, it*).

- That start and end the same (*ball, bell, bill*).

- That feature a particular vowel (words with *a—car, apple, cat, fan, mail*).

- With letter clusters (blends such as *tr—try, tree, trip*).

Figure 8–7 *Magnetic Letters/Words*

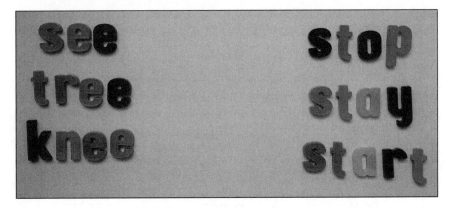

- With letter clusters (digraphs such as *ch*, *wh*, *sh*, and *th*).

- With similar endings (*looking*, *running*, *walked*, *played*, *biggest*, *smallest*).

- With plural endings (*cats*, *dogs*, *wolves*, *ponies*).

- With one syllable (*dog*), two syllables (*rabbit*), three syllables (*kangaroo*).

- With two letters (*up*, *no*, *go*, *it*, *at*, *we*).

- With three letters (*day*, *cat*, *bus*, *mom*).

There are many ways to work with phonics principles. We suggest writing words or building them with magnetic letters. Here are some ways to help your partner explore the phonics principles:

- Place words on cards and invite your partner to sort them; for example, sort words by the number of letters or by the first letter (see Figure 8–8).

- Draw your partner's attention to letters, letter clusters (or groups of letters that often appear together), and endings when she writes them or encounters them in reading.

- Using a little notebook, make a personal dictionary of high-frequency words and also of useful words that your partner has discovered.

- Make a word chart with your partner, putting together words that are alike. (In Figure 8–9, words are sorted according to the "o" sound and the spelling of the "o" sound.)

Finally, there are many commercially available letter and word games that you might enjoy playing with your partner. Often some of these games are on hand in schools, so ask the teacher with whom you work.

Also, if computers are available and you know how to operate one, you can find commercial software to help children learn about phonics. Make

Figure 8–8 *Word Sort*

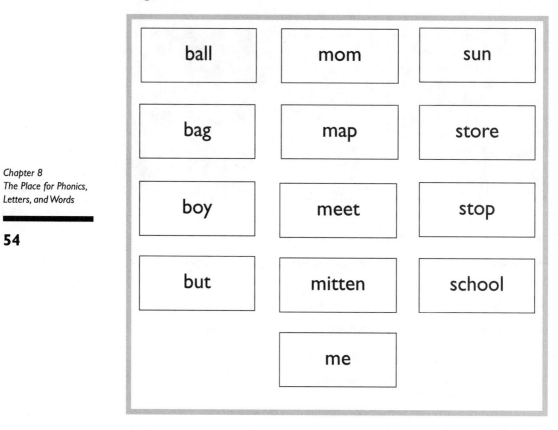

ball	mom	sun
bag	map	store
boy	meet	stop
but	mitten	school
	me	

Figure 8–9 *Word Chart*

Words with O

soap	home	over
goat	pole	open
boat	rope	ocean
	note	
show	cow	out
slow	now	ounce
crow	clown	foul

sure that the tasks are within her grasp and skill range. Excessive drills on phonics material that is too hard does not promote reading and may cause your partner to resent and resist the task. Sit next to her while she plays the computer games so she can request your help if she needs it. This way, she'll get the most from the games.

HELPING CHILDREN READ, WRITE, AND LEARN PHONICS

We described some strategies to help children learn about phonics, but they will learn about letters, sounds, and words every time they open a book or put pen to paper. As children write, they notice letters and the sounds they make and begin to apply this knowledge to reading. They also begin to develop a knowledge of many sight words. These sight words are key because they enable children to read and write new words.

TAKE NOTE

Take a moment to ask yourself,

◆ Are the children learning the alphabet names, letter sounds, and high-frequency words?

◆ Do they use their knowledge of letters, sounds, and words when they read and write stories and messages?

◆ Do they comment on the letters and words they recognize, and connect them to words they know and new words they encounter?

CHAPTER NINE

What About Writing and Spelling?

Learning any new skill takes time. We know from reflecting on our own experiences as learners that it's always easier to learn something new when we have a teacher who is willing to show us how to become skillful, too. Learning a new skill often involves the opportunity to:

- See someone else do it.

- Try it yourself with guidance from someone who knows how to do it.

- Do it by yourself with advice from a knowledgeable person.

- Do it completely alone and feel pride in the results.

Young children who are learning to write need all four kinds of opportunities. That means you'll want to:

- Show children how to write by writing for them.

- Share the writing task, inviting children to contribute what they can.

- Help children as they write for themselves.

- Provide materials and serve as an audience (or reader) of the material children write by themselves.

This chapter explains how to show children what writing is and how it is done. It also describes how to share writing and to assist children as they write and spell on their own.

AN ANALOGY

Think about something you learned to do as a child. Perhaps you learned to care for a garden, build a bookcase, or cook. If you learned to cook, chances are you learned by working alongside the cook of the family while he or she prepared a real meal. Without being conscious of your learning, you probably acquired some general knowledge about cooking:

- How do cooks act? They stir, put things in the oven, serve plates, etc.

- What is the sequence of action? What happens first, second, and so on?

- How do people talk in the kitchen? ("It needs a little salt.")

- How do people share tasks in the kitchen? ("You chop that up and I'll blend it into this.")

If you were around people who cooked, you probably learned enough just by watching to "play cooking." Soon, if you continued to observe in the kitchen, the cook began to involve you in small ways that were easy for you. Maybe the cook invited you to stir something or to measure an ingredient. The cook certainly exercised patience because giving you the task to do took more time and effort and achieved a less perfect result than if the more expert cook completed it.

The advantage, though, is that you learned as you worked. You weren't cooking just to practice—you were actually cooking your family's dinner. The cook handled the hard parts; you managed the easy parts. Gradually, you mastered many more skills so you could work effectively with the cook. The cook didn't need to teach you the easy tasks, only the new ones you were learning.

Finally, you could prepare a whole dinner by yourself with only a little direction from the cook. Each time, from the beginning to the independent work in the kitchen, you had the reward of seeing a whole meal prepared, and those who ate it appreciated the results. The four elements—seeing it, doing it with someone, doing it alone with support, and doing it independently—were all there. The elements apply to this description of learning to cook; they also apply to learning how to service a car, do the laundry, use a computer, or write.

LEARNING ABOUT WRITING

Children should understand the role of writing "mechanics"—putting correctly spelled words together in sentences with punctuation—but they should also understand what writing is for and how people use it in their daily lives. In this section, we explore several areas of learning that apply to all three writing experiences: writing for children, writing with them, and helping them write for themselves.

Understanding the reasons to write

Often, children just "do" writing to complete a school assignment. Real writers, on the other hand, are inspired by real reasons to write. As a literacy volunteer, you can help your partner find real reasons to write, helping him to discover writing as a meaningful experience.

When you share different kinds of books, you expose children to different kinds of writing. For this reason, read aloud a wide variety of reading materials and talk about the kind of writing each represents:

- Alphabet books.
- Books written as letters, diaries, or post cards (*Stringbean's Trip to the Shining Sea*; *Dear Mr. Blueberry*; *Dear Annie*).
- Poems or rhymes.
- Newspaper articles.
- Riddles or cartoons.
- Plays.

Talking about what to write

When a child writes, he has to make a lot of decisions about how to communicate what he wants to say. Clear, effective writing often begins with talking:

- Encourage him to select topics for writing that are interesting and meaningful for him; we all write best about what we know or care about.

- Invite him to talk about his writing to clarify what it is he really wants to say.

- Listen to what your partner is trying to say and then tell him what you heard or understood, asking him questions to clarify.

- Encourage your partner to say his whole message and be sure that the expanded message is really his rather than yours.

WRITING FOR CHILDREN

Writing for children helps them realize that we can write down what we think and say. They'll also discover that writing serves many purposes; in fact, there is almost no limit to the ways in which adults can demonstrate writing for children. As you share these reasons to write with your partner, be sure to read aloud what you write:

- Names of friends or family members.

- Notes, greeting cards, or post cards.

- Letters to friends or family members.

- Lists of things to buy or do.

- Recipes or directions.

- Labels on pictures.

- A scrapbook of special pictures or items with labels.

- Stories your partner tells you.

- Lists of stories you and your partner have read together.

- Summaries of stories you have read together.

- A shared journal to pass back and forth just like a written conversation.

- Webs of information such as the character map in Figure 9–1.

Figure 9–1 *Character Map*

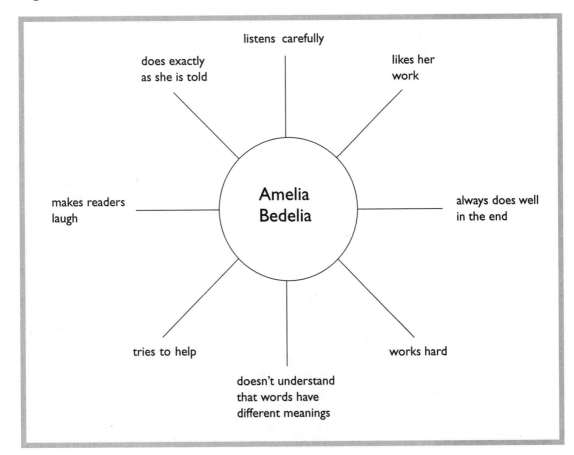

listens carefully

does exactly
as she is told

likes her
work

makes readers
laugh

**Amelia
Bedelia**

always does well
in the end

tries to help

works hard

doesn't understand
that words have
different meanings

Use writing to teach children some of the important details about written language. As you demonstrate writing for the child, he has the opportunity to notice that:

- Writing involves writing letters, left to right, one after another.

- Making words means leaving space between groups of letters.

- Every time you write the same word, it looks the same (it has the same letters).

- Some words appear more often than others.

- There are connections between words and what you know about letters.

- Some words look like other words—they may start with the same letter, look alike in parts, or end with the same letter.

- There is a connection between the sounds you make when you say a word and the letters that you make when you write a word.

- Sometimes one letter makes one sound (*s*). Sometimes more than one letter makes one sound (*ch*).

What sort of writing might you do for children? If you are working in a classroom, you might write children's dictated stories or write labels to explain the pictures. Here are some suggestions that will help you be more effective when you write for children:

- Sit beside the child (instead of across from) so that both of you can easily see what you are writing, or write on an easel that both of you can see.

- Print clearly using a standard form for letters. If you are working in a classroom, ask the teacher for the preferred form of print and use it. This will make it easier for the child to read.

- Write in lowercase forms, using capitals in a standard way at the beginning of sentences, for proper names, etc. Books are printed in upper- and lowercase letters and children need to understand the role of both.

- Talk over the message or story with the child before you start to write it. Ask the child to compose a whole sentence so that you establish the general meaning of the story. This helps the young child learn that when you write, you should have in mind a whole message, or at least a meaningful part of one.

- If it's difficult to help the child think of something to write, initiate a conversation about something that interests him (see Chapter 3). As he talks, listen for possible writing topics and suggest, when you hear one, "That would be great to write about!"

- Shape the message a little if necessary; that is, put it into words that are easier to read. Very young children may talk on and on without realizing that not everything they say sounds "right" written down. We also want the child to be able to read it. A long, rambling message will be too difficult to read.

- Be sure to use the child's own words instead of your more "grammatical" or "literary" version. The purpose of writing for children is to demonstrate the process, not to change their language. As the child hears more written language and gains experience, he will learn how written language sounds. Many volunteers find that even very young children who have been read to a lot dictate sentences that sound like book language.

- As you write, make comments about the message. Say the words slowly (although not in a distorted way) as you write them. You might say, for example, in a conversational way, "I need a space." Or, "I don't have enough room. I'll have to go down to the next line."

- Reread the message frequently. For young children, reread it every time you add a new word, going back to the beginning and pointing as you read each word, right up to the space for the next new word you will write.

- Draw the child's attention to the connections between letters and sounds. For example, "*Sun* . . . that starts with *s*."

- Draw the child's attention to the letters and words that may be familiar to him, for example, "*Ball* . . . that starts like your name [or the name of someone else in the class]."

- Comment on punctuation as you use it.

Your writing makes valuable material your partner will enjoy reading and rereading.

WRITING WITH CHILDREN

Teachers call writing with children "shared writing" or "interactive writing." It encourages children to take a more active role in the writing process. Here is a brief definition:

> In interactive writing, the adult and child work together first to compose a message. Then they write it, sharing the pen so that the child can use his growing knowledge of the forms of writing.

When you write *with* your partner, let him write everything he can, and then you fill in the rest. It is not a matter of correcting your partner; the whole process is shared. We recommend that you work with one child. If you have a group, keep it small. Assist no more than three children at a time.

To make shared writing effective, you need to know your partner. That way, by knowing which letters he can identify or write, you can involve him at just the right time.

Figure 9–2 is an example of a piece of interactive writing produced by six-year-old Sharra and literacy volunteer Helen.

Figure 9–2 *Sharra's First Writing*

This message is simple, one of a whole series of messages created for Sharra's "I like" book. Here is the process they used:

1. First, Helen and Sharra decided what they would write and said it several times so they could remember it. Remembering a message is something that Sharra needs to learn so that she can, eventually, sustain the meaning of her writing even as she works through the somewhat tedious process of forming letters to create words.

2. Then, Helen invited Sharra to write the word *I*. She had written this word several times before. The same was true for *like* and *to*. Through shared reading and interactive writing, Sharra was building up a few words that she knew in every detail. This interactive writing time gave her a chance to produce them.

3. Each time Sharra wrote a word, they reread the message, pointing under the words.

4. The next word was *eat*, which was not a familiar word to Sharra. Helen invited her to say it slowly, and showed her how. She made sure that Sharra said the word herself. After saying the word a couple of times, Sharra said, "I hear *e*."

5. "That's right," Helen said, "It does have an *e*. You can write it here."

6. After Sharra wrote the *e*, Helen wrote the rest of the word. Then, they reread the first four words of the message, which helped Sharra think of the next word, *peanut*.

7. Again, Helen invited Sharra to say the word slowly and to think about the letters that might be in it. For both *peanut* and *butter*, Sharra could think of the first letter and write it and Helen wrote the rest. Each time, they reread the message.

8. For the word *and*, when asked to say it slowly, Sharra could think of the *a* and the *d*. It is unlikely that she really knew the vowel sound *a*, but producing it shows that she had some knowledge of the word. She clearly heard the *d* at the end. Helen filled in the middle letter.

9. Helen wrote the final word, *jelly*, and, again, they reread the message. Part of the adult's skill in interactive writing is knowing when to write for the child so that the task does not become too tedious.

10. They read the message many times while they created it. It also became part of a book that they made together and then used as reading material.

Two weeks later, Sharra and Helen wrote the message in Figure 9–3.

Figure 9–3   *Sharra's Writing*

This message shows that Sharra was building more writing power. She wrote all by herself *I like to go to see my*. She heard the sounds and wrote the first three letters of *granny* and the first letter of *sometimes*. At this point, we can see that Sharra is still trying to control the forms of the letters, but it is getting easier for her to do so. Her partner helped her think how to form the letters and practice them. She is mixing capital and small letters, but the adult can prompt her to use lowercase forms. Sharra is doing the parts that are possible for her to do; the adult is doing the hard parts, just like in the cooking lesson. The progress will continue. Just a few days later, Sharra wrote the entire word *granny*.

The process of thinking of the message or story is very much like that described above in the section on writing for children, but in interactive writing, it is even more important to create a message that you and your partner can read. The suggestions for how to write are the same.

Here are some additional suggestions for working with children as you "share the pen":

- Be sure that your partner creates the message. For the experience to be successful, the language must be his.

- Reread the message every time you add a new word. Invite your partner to reread with you and point under each word.

- Don't ask your partner to write something for every word. Pick out several words you know he can write or partially write. The first and last letters of a word are usually the easiest for the child.

- Then, invite him to say these words slowly with you.

- Accept the child's contributions as indicators of learning. Let's say he wants to use the word *after*. He says, "I hear *r*!" In this situation, you would say, "You're right. There is an *r*. You would then write *afte*, letting him write the *r*.

- Sometimes children can think of the letter associated with a sound but they are not able to write it on the paper. In this case, just write the letter for the child quickly and let him copy it. Or, you can guide his attempt by helping him do each part of the letter (see Chapter 8).

- Be sure to praise the child's every attempt. Writing is difficult for the beginner.

- Be sure to use correct spelling at the end. You are there to fill in the letters that children do not know. The piece of writing, then, will be good material for the child to read again and again.

When children write on their own, in the early stages, they will misspell words. We don't want to discourage them from writing by correcting everything they attempt. Gradually, they will learn to spell many words without having to think about it. They will also begin to discover rules that will help them spell new words. Interactive writing helps you help children learn more about spelling.

Both processes—writing for children and writing with children—provide young writers with the adult support they need as they begin to write. The goal is independent writing and spelling. As you work with a child over time, you will notice that he is learning more and offering to do more. He is gaining confidence, but he is also gaining skill. For example, you might hear, "I can write that!" Or, "I know that word!" You'll want to hold back and let him try on his own.

Remember to praise and appreciate that the child is:

- Trying something that is (or was) hard for him.

- Using what he knows.

- Getting at least part of the word "right."

When you praise a child, be specific. "I like the way you said the word slowly and thought about it." Or, "I like the way you made your *s*." Children need specific encouragement for what they do well and clear demonstrations of what they still need to learn.

One of the joys of writing is that when it is finished, you and the child will have something you can hold and read, giving you both a sense of pride and accomplishment. Self-esteem is built through daily accomplishments. Writing offers even a beginner the opportunity to experience success.

HELPING CHILDREN WRITE

By writing for your partner and writing with him, you help him prepare to write for himself. With your help, he can write on his own. You provide just enough help so that he is successful and does more than he could do all alone.

Be careful not to overwhelm the young writer and make writing a tedious task. Every time the child produces a piece of writing and is proud of his efforts, he will build his skills.

Writing to learn skills

As they write, children learn the skills or "mechanics of writing" that enable others to read their writing. In other words, children learn spelling, punctuation, and grammar as they use them to convey a message. Before you and your partner attend to the mechanics, however, help him decide on a message complex enough to challenge him but simple enough that he can write it successfully. Don't try to do too much in a single sitting. If your partner's idea or message is too long, write part of it one day and the rest another day, rereading each time to remember it. Remember that drawings communicate meaning to readers, too. You'll want to notice and encourage your partner's illustrations. Once your partner is clear about what he wants to say, you can shift your attention to the mechanics that will enable others to read his message:

- Encourage your partner to use the words that he can see around him, such as on a word list posted on a wall or in poems displayed on a blackboard. You might also show your partner how to use a simple dictionary.

- Encourage your partner to take "risks" and stretch himself developmentally as a writer. Your job is to accept what he can do even if it is not perfect.

- Help your partner problem solve as he attempts to spell new words. He can "work it out" by saying words slowly, examining what looks right, or remembering other words like the one he wants to write.

- Encourage your partner to read and reread what he has written. Rereading will help him notice more about the printed message. He will start to self-correct.

- Don't overwhelm your partner with corrections. Children can only focus on a few new understandings at a time.

Helping the beginning writer

Beginning writers are just becoming writers. Let's consider everything a new writer needs to know about what writing is and what writing does. The beginning writer needs to understand that:

- Symbols or marks on a page convey a message.

- Print is made up of letter symbols and punctuation marks.

- The print is written left to right across the page and starts again on the left.

- Words are one letter or a group of letters; white space is on either side of a word.

- Letters or groups of letters have sounds.

- Some letters are called capital or "uppercase" letters; others are small or "lowercase" letters.

- Punctuation marks tell the reader to stop (period), take a breath (comma), to read like talking (quotation marks), to read with excitement (exclamation mark), or to raise one's voice as in a question (question mark).

To help your partner understand how these writing skills support effective writing, you should:

- Talk about letters, words, and punctuation as you help the child write.

- Count the number of words the child wants to write in a sentence and discuss the spacing between each.

- Invite the child to reread what he has written to decide what to write next.

- Help the child to think about what sounds he hears and what letter or letters he should write to match the sounds.

- Help the child think about the small words or high-frequency words he knows how to write.

You won't need many of these suggestions once the child is able to write more on his own.

Helping the developing writer

The developing writer is a little more experienced than the beginning writer. In fact, the developing writer can begin to reread his writing and check to make sure that everything that *should* be there *is* there. Let us explain.

The child's first attempt to write is called a "draft." As the child reads and rereads his draft, he will make changes and notice words that need fixing. This is called "proofreading"—the final writing step. Your partner should read the draft one more time to check that he has done everything he knows how to do. This doesn't mean that everything will be correct, but he will begin to learn the important skill of proofreading. Use the following questions to help your partner check what he has written:

- Has your partner said what he wants his readers to know?

- Has he presented the information in a logical order?

- Does he convey the information in an interesting way?

- Could he cut excess information and compose a tighter, more focused draft?

Next, help your partner consider the mechanics of his writing. These expectations will vary for each child and grade level, so, if possible, check with your partner's teacher to know more about what is expected.

- Has he written the words legibly?

- Has he left space between the words?

- Has he written some words correctly? How many?

- Of the misspelled words your partner attempted to write, did he spell some nearly right? Does he know some simple words that he can fix easily?

- Are there two or three words your partner can circle that he would like to learn to write correctly? Help the child say these words slowly and think about how they would look.

- Has the child used punctuation to tell the reader when to come to a full stop (period), pause (comma), or raise one's voice (question mark)?

- Has the child understood the form needed for the writing (for example, a letter, directions, or a story form)?

LEARNING ABOUT SPELLING

Spelling helps readers follow what the writer is trying to say. Young children are just learning how to write the words of the language. It will take many years to develop a large writing vocabulary of words they know how to spell correctly. Very few people can spell all the words of their language correctly. What matters is that, as we write, we continually get better at spelling words. We learn how to try words when we are stuck. We also learn how to use references such as dictionaries.

Helping children learn spelling principles

In the first years of school, children need to learn three key principles that will help them learn to write new words (Clay 1991). Help children use these principles to write words whenever you can:

1. When you say words slowly, you can listen for the sounds you hear and you can write them (*dog, man*).

2. You can think about how words look as you try to write them (*make, should*).

3. If you think of other words that are like the word you are trying to write, it will help you write a new word. For example, if you want to write *stay*, you can think of a word that starts like it (*stop*) and ends like it (*day*). Using the parts you know from other words helps you to write new words.

Helping children learn to spell useful words

Help the children think about frequently occurring words and keep a list of ones they are learning to write. You may want to begin a list arranged by the initial letter, such as the one in Figure 9–4. You can tape the list on the wall or place a sheet in the child's writing folder.

When your partner rereads his writing, ask him to crosscheck his writing against his list and search for the words he knows. If he has misspelled any of the words in his writing that he has written correctly on his list, he should correct the misspellings.

Helping children spell new words

When you help your partner try different ways to spell a word, he is learning to focus more closely on its features. *Have a try* is a technique that

Figure 9–4

WORDS I KNOW HOW TO WRITE			
Aa at am and	Bb but	Cc can	Dd did
Ee eat	Ff for from	Gg go get	Hh he his him
Ii I is in it	Jj	Kk keep	Ll let look
Mm me my	Nn no	Oo on	Pp put
Qq	Rr read	Ss so said	Tt to them the they
Uu up	Vv	Ww we was	Xx Yy Zz you yes

works well for the slightly more capable writer (see Figure 9–5). This is how it works:

1. The child circles or underlines words in his story that he is not sure about.
2. The child chooses two or three he'd like to learn how to spell.
3. The child writes them in the left column of the chart, tries two or three different spellings, and circles the one that looks right. This is repeated for each word.
4. Finally, the child checks the words with a dictionary or an adult and fixes them in his writing.

Another useful technique to help children learn to spell new words is *Look, Say, Cover, Write, Check* (see Figure 9–6). This is how it works:

Figure 9–5

HAVE A TRY				
First Try	Second Try	Third Try	Correct Spelling	Copy
Scool	skool	shcool	school	school
ware	whare	waer	where	where
becus	becaus	because	because	because

Figure 9–6 *Look-Say-Cover-Write-Check Chart*

	have	have	have
1. Look and Say	they	they	they
2. Cover and Write	brother	brother	brother
3. Check	was	Was	was
	said	said	said

1. The writer lists the words he wants to learn in the left column of the chart.

2. The writer *looks* at each word carefully, *saying* it and thinking about what will help him remember how to write it.

3. The writer uses a card to *cover* the word on the left and *write* it in the next column.

4. The writer uncovers and *checks* the word.

5. The writer repeats this process two or three times until he feels he knows the word well.

Children become effective spellers as they use what they know to check themselves.

TAKE NOTE

From time to time ask yourself some questions about what happens when you help children write:

◆ Does my partner enjoy writing, and do I remember to praise his efforts?

◆ Is he focusing on the message of his writing before he attends to the writing mechanics?

◆ Is my partner learning one or two new things that help him as a writer each time we work together, and is he clearly making progress?

◆ Is he thinking of topics to write about, or do I need to prompt him?

◆ Does my partner seem to understand his role when I write for him (for example, I write while he watches; then he helps me reread)?

◆ Does my partner seem to understand his role in shared writing (for example, he says each word slowly as I prompt him, and he takes the pen and fills in letters or words he knows)?

◆ Is he increasingly able to hear the sounds in words when he says them slowly, and is he building up a group of words that he knows and can write easily?

◆ Is my partner doing more of the writing, and is he creating longer, more complex sentences or messages?

◆ Is he proud of his writing efforts? Will he draw a picture, read his writing to someone, or take it home?

CHAPTER TEN

Make Your Own Book!

Everyone loves a book and young children are no exception, especially when it's a book they've written and created themselves. It's hard to beat the sheer pleasure and learning success inherent in the simple joy of creating one's own book (see Figure 10–1). Little handmade books are simple, readable stories that combine reading and writing. There are three ways to help children make books. You can write books for children, demonstrating the process. You can write books with children. Or you can help them as they write their own. The result is a book that the child can read for herself even if she is a beginner. We find that children like to keep and reread, again and again, the books that they make with volunteers.

WRITING BOOKS FOR CHILDREN

Children love to see and read books made especially for them. You might write the book at home and bring it to share with your partner. Or you might have a book in mind and write it while your partner watches you. That way, she can see exactly how the book is made from start to finish. We provide instructions for book making later in this chapter.

Writing a book for your partner shouldn't be daunting. Try these suggestions:

- Think about the child's interests and make a book about that topic.

- Make the book to share something about yourself (such as a book about your pet).

Figure 10–1

VALUES OF BOOK MAKING	
Values of Book Making for Reading	**Values of Book Making for Writing**
Children enjoy reading these little books again and again.	Children enjoy using their writing skills to make a book.
As they begin to read, children need many experiences to read simple books. These books are inexpensive and offer the chance to read and reread many words.	The children have the opportunity to think of a whole story and put it together, page after page.
Because the books are so easy and familiar, children can focus on the meaning of the story while beginning to notice the details of print.	As they make a little book, children learn important understandings (such as the meaning of a title, how to read left to right through the book, etc.).
Children can practice looking at the illustrations for information and try to match them with the language of the book and print.	Book making enables children to make connections between letters and sounds.
Children can practice using the pictures and/or print to check on themselves while reading.	Book making enables children to practice writing and spelling words while they experience the pride of creating a book.
Children will have the opportunity to practice early skills such as word by word matching and moving left to right across print or through a book.	Making a book is a whole experience that combines reading and writing and helps young children understand the connections between the two.

- Use your partner's name in the book (for example, "Maria likes to eat cereal.").

- For children who are just beginning to read, use only one or two lines of print. For more advanced children, adjust the text so it's more challenging, but be careful not to make it too hard.

- If your partner can read only a few words, find ways to use those words in the book (for example, *the* or *is*: "I see the ball."

- Select clear pictures that support the text and are easy for your partner to understand.

Sharing the pen

Although your partner will delight in reading the books you write for her, she will also enjoy coauthoring a book with you. As you work together on the book, your partner can write in the words and letters that she knows. Here are some tips to get you started:

- Have in mind some possible topics and sentences to help your partner begin.

- Talk together to decide what the book will be about. You do not have to make up every page of the entire book before you start, but you should have an overall idea.

- Preselect some pictures for the book. Cut the pictures from magazines, newspapers, catalogs, or any other source. You can also draw pictures, invite your partner to draw, or make drawings together. Book making is different, however, from an art activity. Since you want these books to be read again and again, your partner may need some help to create identifiable pictures that match and support the text.

- Write the book, one page at a time, sharing the pen. Use the handwriting chart in Chapter 8 for a model.

- You might begin with the child's name. After all, that's one word the child can almost certainly write, at least in part.

- Reread the whole book each time you start to write a new page so that your partner can remember the pattern or theme of the book.

- Keep the books you write together in a special place.

Helping children write books

After your partner has authored several books with your help, she will want to write a book all by herself. Your role is to observe her and help as needed. Here's what you can do:

- Give your partner a collection of pictures that she can use to select pictures for her book. Some volunteers have envelopes of cut-out pictures from magazines, catalogs, or newspapers on different topics (for example, animals, food, toys, families, sports, holiday decorations, etc.). Sometimes just looking through these pictures can give your partner an idea for a book.

- Have supplies available and ready to use.

- Watch your partner as she works on her book. Encourage her to write words she doesn't know. Use the approaches we explain in Chapter 9.

- Encourage the child to reread while writing each page and to reread the whole book.

- Store the book in a special place so your partner can read and enjoy it whenever she wishes.

WHAT IT TAKES TO MAKE A BOOK

What do you need to make a book? With just a few basic materials, you can create an impressive little book:

- Paper—average or heavy weight—8½-by-11-inch sheets and other sizes.

- Scissors.

- Glue or paste.

- Pictures to select (from magazines, newspapers, catalogs, stickers, etc.).

- A stapler.

- Thin markers, such as Crayola washables or any dark markers (eliminate light yellow or orange because the print is too hard to see).

- Crayons or other materials for drawing.

Be careful that the writing on the back of one page does not "bleed through" to the other side. Seeing the print from the other side is very confusing to a young reader. Thicker paper will solve this problem. Also, look for Crayola markers because they tend not to bleed through. If you have to use thin paper, write on a separate piece of paper that you've pasted to another sheet for double thickness. You can also place white Post-it tape on a page and then write on it.

FINDING IDEAS FOR BOOKS

Books can spring to life from any topic that is of interest to you and the child. In general, for young readers, very easy books on simple topics work best. Figure 10–2 shows two pages from a homemade book.

In this example, the print is clear and easy to read. It is not too small and not too large. There are clear spaces between words. These spaces are a little larger than usual; they make it easy for the child to point to

Figure 10–2 *Two Pages of a Tutor-Made Book:* My Neighborhood

Here is my house.

Figure 10–3 *Two Pages of a Tutor-Made Book:* I Can See

the words while reading. The pictures provide an idea about what the print will say. There is a complete sentence on each page, and the sentences are easy ones for the child to predict. This book is very easy; it has only one line of print.

The example in Figure 10–3 is a little harder. There are two lines of print, and the sentences are longer. Notice, though, that each sentence begins on a new line, making it easier for the child to return to the left for a new sentence. The topics of both books are familiar to young children.

Why don't you try making your own book? Figure 10–4 provides directions to get you started.

Patterns to write by

Designing little books helps children understand how sentences and stories can be captured in print. Suggest some basic language patterns for the beginner. You won't need to use such patterns once the child becomes a more accomplished reader and writer, but they will help you get started.

Use personal pronouns, common objects, and children's names in very simple language patterns. Children can write about what they see around the classroom or school or they can use common objects such as toys. Increase the challenge by lengthening sentences or by changing the language pattern at the end.

- I like _____. (This is one of the easiest patterns!) Increase the challenge by ending the last page with "What do you like?" (Use colors, activities, food, etc.)

- We like _____. We like to _____.

- (Name) likes _____. (Name) likes to _____. (You have many options here, for example, "eat," "play with," or any kind of action.)

- Here is a _____. This is _____. This is a _____.

Figure 10–4

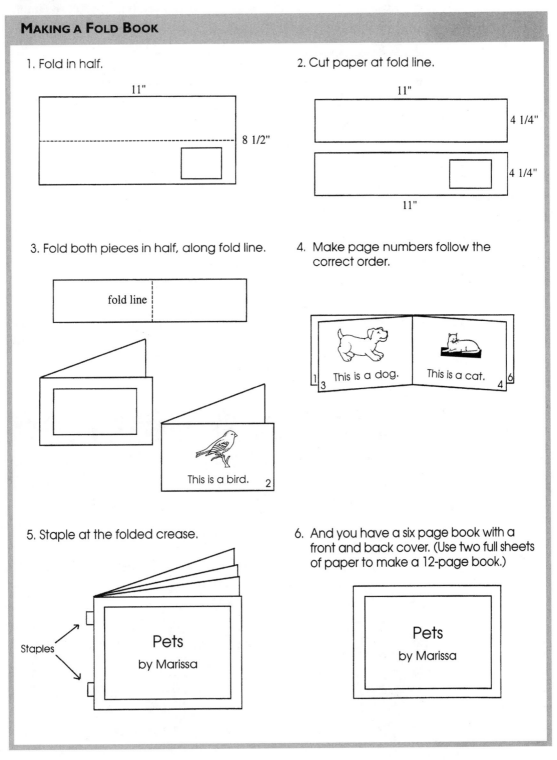

MAKING A FOLD BOOK

1. Fold in half.

11"

8 1/2"

2. Cut paper at fold line.

11"

4 1/4"

4 1/4"

11"

3. Fold both pieces in half, along fold line.

fold line

This is a bird.   2

4. Make page numbers follow the correct order.

1
3   This is a dog.   This is a cat.   4   6

5. Staple at the folded crease.

Staples

Pets
by Marissa

6. And you have a six page book with a front and back cover. (Use two full sheets of paper to make a 12-page book.)

Pets
by Marissa

- I can _____. Mom (or any name) is _____. (Use action words.)
- I can see _____. I can see a _____. I can see the _____. (Use familiar objects.)

Use questions and answers.

- Where is _____ (name or animal)? Is she (or he) in the _____?
- Do you like _____ (food or any kind of activity)? Yes! (Or no!)
- Can (name) _____? Yes, he (or she) can.

Use dialogue.

- "I like _____," said (name).
- "I like to eat _____," said (name).
- "Let's go swimming (or any other activity)," said (name). "No, it's too cold," said (name).
- "I want to go to (store or fast-food restaurant)," said (name). (Name) ate some ice cream, but it was too cold.

Reading children's literature will give you many more ideas. For example, books such as *Fortunately, Unfortunately* by Remy Charlip, *How Many Bugs in a Box?* by David Carter, and *The Important Book* by Margaret Wise Brown provide lively language formats that children can model in their own books.

TAKE NOTE

It's hard to beat becoming the author of your own little book. Here are some things to think about as you help your young author:

- ◆ Am I building a collection of handmade books that my partner can read alone or with assistance?
- ◆ Do we write about different topics, using different language patterns and experimenting with different "genres" (stories, poems, reports, etc.)?
- ◆ Does my partner offer ideas for the storyline and does she volunteer to write the letters and words she knows?
- ◆ Do my partner and I reread each new book as we make it? Do we reread books that we've made before and that have become favorites?
- ◆ Do the books in our collection give my partner a chance to read many high-frequency words?
- ◆ Does my partner volunteer to read the handmade books in her collection, and is she eager to take our handmade books home to show her family?
- ◆ Does she look forward to writing another book with me?

CHAPTER ELEVEN

Make a Difference at Home

We have long known that positive literacy experiences in *both* home and school help children succeed. A strong partnership between home and school, then, is our goal, but it requires time and effort. Can you play a role in supporting home literacy? Absolutely! You can help by finding simple ways to make it easier for the child and his family to become involved in literacy at home.[1]

In this chapter we suggest practical ideas that you can do every day—ideas that don't require many resources. In the guide for volunteer coordinators that accompanies this handbook, we offer detailed descriptions of more extensive projects that groups of volunteers can try.

ENCOURAGING CHILDREN TO EXPLORE WRITING AT HOME

Children need a chance to experiment with writing at home. Without the pressure of school assignments, they can practice everything they have learned and, in the process, improve their writing ability. Sometimes parents do not fully understand or appreciate how their children can benefit from writing at

---

[1]If you are working in a school, policies require that you plan any home contacts with the teacher and sometimes the principal. Before you send materials home with children, check with the school.

home. They may think that pencils are dangerous (and they can be if not used properly) or that children need to copy so that they can "get it right." They may think that children should not write until they can do it perfectly.

Seeing is often believing—as parents witness their children in action as writers and the exciting writing that results, they will realize how writing helps their children become stronger readers. The following section offers some simple suggestions for promoting writing at home.

COMMUNICATING CLEARLY AND OFTEN

If you are working in a school, check with the teacher before you send anything home with the child. Remember that some teachers prefer to communicate with parents themselves. If you have the teacher's approval, however, you can write brief, handwritten notes to parents that explain the sort of writing their children might do (see Figures 11–1, 11–2, and 11–3).

Figure 11–1 Note Home to Parents

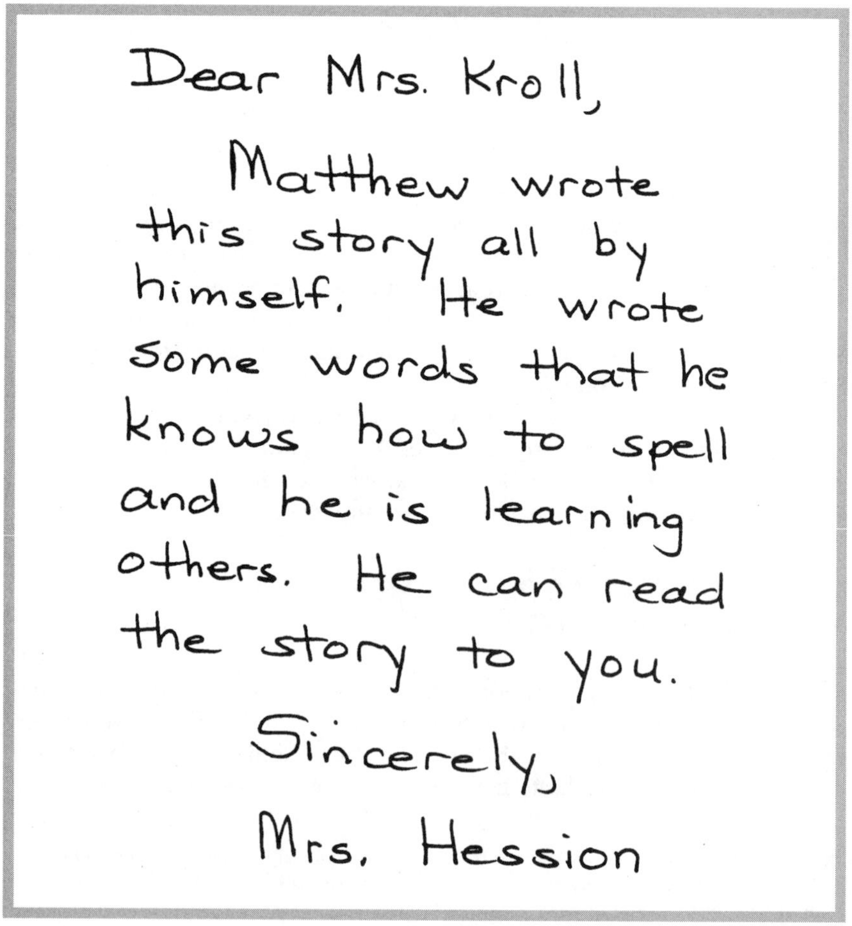

Dear Mrs. Kroll,

Matthew wrote this story all by himself. He wrote some words that he knows how to spell and he is learning others. He can read the story to you.

Sincerely,

Mrs. Hession

Figure 11–2 *Note Home to Parents*

Dear Mrs. Law,
Aneeca and I made this book together. It's about all the things she likes. She wrote the words I and like, and I wrote the rest. She is learning about letters and sounds. I know you will enjoy reading this book with her.

Sincerely,
Mr. Thomas

Sending home materials

Send home simple materials and expect writing back the next day. You do not need to have elaborate plans to increase the writing resources in children's homes. With just a little effort, you can encourage children to write at home:

- Send home a folded piece of paper in an envelope or a plastic storage bag along with a pen or marker. It is a good idea to put the bag or envelope in the child's school bag while the child is watching and to talk about why you are doing it. The plastic bag makes it much more likely that the child will preserve the materials and bring back a written story the next day, and you can reuse the bag.

Figure 11–3 *Note Home to Parents*

Dear Mr. Peters,

I am sending home paper so that Maria can make a book at home like the ones we have been making at school.

Ms. Rodriguez

- Cut a picture or pictures from a newspaper or magazine and paste them on a sheet of paper or into a short four-page book, leaving blank space for the child to write underneath. Let the child take the book home in the plastic bag and write in it with the help of family members.

- Prefold and staple a blank book for the child to take home.

- See if local businesses will offer free pens that you can include with paper. Even young children can use a variety of writing implements such as ballpoint pens, markers, crayons, and pencils. If you send home a pencil, be sure that it is sharpened and that the child knows how to use it properly and safely.

- Help children make little "notebooks"; they love them! They are easy to make by stapling together several small pieces of paper. You can also fold index cards to make greeting cards or notes. Add stickers, stars, or colored drawings for easy sparkle!

- Check out used or discarded office supplies for an abundant source of home literacy materials. Cut up old mailing envelopes and use the backs for children's writing material. Used large brown or manila envelopes make nice, stiff writing material. Fold them to make cards or use them as frames for pictures.

- Pay special attention to any writing your partner does at home. If you are not present the day he brings it in, he should know to store it in a special place and save it for you to look at when you return. Children become inspired authors when they experience success with home writing. They want to write!

■ Praise your partner for any writing he does at home, but don't chastise him if he doesn't return the materials. Sometimes it's quite difficult for young children to follow through on a home assignment.

Explaining the writing materials

Be sure your partner understands the purpose for the writing materials you send home. Model for the child what you want him to do with writing materials that you send home. It is a good idea to practice the task many times at school (for example, thinking of a message and then beginning to write it; folding paper to make a book; making a picture and then labeling it, etc.) before sending home writing materials. If the child knows just what to do, his family members will feel more secure and will let him take the lead.

Sending writing materials home also shows parents the value of home writing. Once family members see their children write using the materials you send home, they may come to understand the value of writing. Following your lead, they may provide their children with materials for writing at home.

ENCOURAGING CHILDREN TO BUILD A HOME LIBRARY

Many beginning readers do have books at home, but they are often difficult stories that adults must read to them. Some of the children's books that you can buy at a grocery store, for instance, can be much too hard for beginners.

The more books children have at home, the more likely it is that they will read. More books plus greater interaction with books equals increased literacy development. So almost anything you can do to help your partner create a home library promotes literacy. It's clear that we want to get books into children's hands. The following section explains how to do it.

Lending books to children

Most schools have libraries. Additionally, classrooms often have books that children are allowed to borrow. Taking home and returning books to a classroom library requires skillful management. If you are working in a school, you can help the teacher organize book borrowing and returning. If you are working in another setting, try to organize the available resources to create a small lending library. Perhaps with contributions from friends or business associates, you can create a small library of paperback books that the children you tutor (or even the entire class) can borrow from and read.

Making or purchasing inexpensive little books that children can keep at home

Children love little books that they can call their own and keep at home. Here are some ways to send those books home:

- If you write books for children (see Chapter 10), you might want to photocopy them and invite the children to take them home for their permanent collections.

- Consider giving the children some short paperback books that are donated to your tutoring program. Children like to put their names in a book and know it's theirs.

- Look for collections of very inexpensive books that are available for groups of volunteers to use with children. Children can also take these books home. Some school districts and community agencies publish their own books that feature local place names and people written into the story line. In the coordinator's guide, we describe a comprehensive KEEP BOOK program.[2]

Once your partner has a collection of books to take home, where will he store them? Here's a handy way to help. First, find a small box (such as a shoe box). Then, keep the box at school for the first few weeks you work with your partner so that you are sure he knows how to use it. He should keep the box in a special place and practice taking books out, reading them, and putting them back in the box. Several different kinds of books may be kept in a book box. Once he knows how to use his storage box, he can take it home to use as his home library.

Finding good books

When we think about books, we think of libraries. It's no surprise, then, that one of your first steps as a literacy volunteer is to locate the local library. Get materials from the library to send to children's homes[3] or write an information sheet for families. Check with your local bookstores, too. Sometimes they are willing to provide free books, give discounts, or notify you of sales.

Book clubs are also a source of inexpensive books. They will send you monthly catalogs at no cost and you may find some books that the school,

---

[2]KEEP BOOKS is a program developed by researchers at The Ohio State University. Children are provided with a series of short, inexpensive (25¢ each) books that are specially designed to support beginning reading strategies. Books have black-and-white illustrations and come in sets of eight titles. These books are distributed on a not-for-profit basis and are intended to be provided by school districts, parent/teacher organizations, and supportive agencies to provide weekly free books for children. A guide is provided to show adults how to use the program; many ideas from this guide are included in this handbook and in the coordinator's guide. For more information, contact The Ohio State University Early Literacy Learning Initiative, 200 Ramseyer Hall, 29 W. Woodruff, Columbus, Ohio 43210; Phone (614) 292-2909; Fax (614) 292-4260.

[3]If you are working in a school, policies require that you show the classroom teacher (and sometimes the principal) any material before you send it to the children's homes.

community organization, or parents can afford to buy. Here is a list of the most popular book clubs and information about how to reach them:

Scholastic Book Club
PO Box 7503
Jefferson City, MO 65102

Troll Book Club
2 Lethbridge Plaza
Mahwah, NJ 07430
1-800-541-1097

Giving your young partner literacy materials to take home supports everything you are doing as a literacy volunteer. In this way, you can build positive connections between home, school, and the other community centers. It's truly a magical moment when a child is able to read and write for and with his family.

TAKE NOTE

Occasionally, you'll want to consider how you can encourage reading and writing in your partner's home:

◆ Does my partner say he's reading books at home?

◆ When I give my partner a book to take home and keep, is he excited? Does he want to read it right away and then reread it? Does he remember to take it home? Does he say that he keeps his books in his book box?

◆ Do children say they read their books to family members?

◆ Do parents tell me that their children are enjoying the books they take home?

◆ Do children use the writing materials to create their own writing at home, and do they return the writing materials?

◆ Do children bring in notes, stories, and messages that they have written at home? Is their home writing improving in length and quality?

◆ Do parents comment that their children are writing at home?

CHAPTER TWELVE

Plan Well to Work Well

Good plans and organized materials will serve you well as you work to serve children. In this last chapter, we provide several sample plans for volunteer tutoring. In addition, we describe a "volunteer tool kit" that will help you organize your resources for the important work you do with children.

SAMPLE PLANS FOR WORKING WITH CHILDREN

Consider your own commitment of time—daily and weekly. Then create an efficient plan for accomplishing as much as possible during that time.

We provide thirty- and forty-five-minute plans for working with young children (Figures 12–1 through 12–8). Use these plans to establish a simple, varied routine for your partner. You can modify the plans in a variety of ways and adjust them to fit your needs. All of the activities we mention in these sample plans are found in this handbook.

Think of the plans as guidelines that you can put together to suit your own needs and purposes as well as those of your partner. How long should you work with your partner? You can determine the right work period by observing the child closely. If she seems distracted after just a few minutes, don't push it, but gradually lengthen the time you can engage her interest. As she learns how to pay attention to her learning experiences with you, she will improve her academic achievement in general.

Figure 12–1

SAMPLE PLAN #1 (30 MINUTES)	
Activity	Approximate Time in Minutes
Select a book and read to the child.	10
Talk with the child about the book.	2
Listen to the child reread several books that she has read in classroom instruction.	8
Reread a favorite that you and the child have read together before. Invite the child to join in on familiar parts. Do it twice if there is time.	5
Write a sentence together about the story.	5

Figure 12–2

SAMPLE PLAN #2 (30 MINUTES)	
Activity	Approximate Time in Minutes
Listen to the child reread several books that she has heard in classroom instruction.	10
Ask the child to choose one or two books and reread them.	5
Introduce a new book and read it with the child. Ask the child to draw the part she likes best. Write a dictated sentence below the child's picture. We recommend that you occasionally use the little, inexpensive books that children can keep. These are described in Chapter 11.	10
Talk about what the child will do with the book at home.	5

Figure 12–3

SAMPLE PLAN #3 (30 MINUTES)	
Activity	Approximate Time in Minutes
Reread some favorite books that you have read aloud before. Invite the child to join in on familiar parts and to talk about the books.	10
Select a new book to read aloud and read it to the child.	10
Write a story summary or reaction to the book you just read.	10

Figure 12–4

SAMPLE PLAN #4 (30 MINUTES)	
Activity	Approximate Time in Minutes
Ask the child to reread several books in her book box (a decorated shoe box or cereal box with the child's name on it). Some of the books might be ones that she has written.	10
Talk with the child to get an idea for a new book to write.	5
Make a book with the child. If there is not enough time to finish the book, do it the next time you are working together. Be sure to reread what was written before ending the session. When you've finished the book, place it with others in her book box.	15

Figure 12–5

SAMPLE PLAN #5 (30 MINUTES)	
Activity	**Approximate Time in Minutes**
Read a book aloud to the child. This might be a favorite book that she has heard before or a new selection.	8
Invite the child to make a book like the one you read. Talk about what you might say in the book.	2
Make the book, rereading each page as you add words and rereading from the beginning each time you add a page. Paste on pictures or help the child draw them.	20

Figure 12–6

SAMPLE PLAN #6 (45 MINUTES)	
Activity	**Approximate Time in Minutes**
Read a book aloud to the child. This might be a new selection or a favorite book that has been read before.	10
Listen to the child read several books from her book box.	10
Work on building words (see Chapter 8, on phonics).	10
Assist the child in writing a page for her journal. Reread what is written. Write a response to what the child has written for her to read.	15

Figure 12–7

SAMPLE PLAN #7 (45 MINUTES)	
Activity	Approximate Time in Minutes
Ask the child to reread the books in her book box.	10
Invite the child to make another book and talk about it.	5
Make a book, rereading each page and the whole book.	15
Work on building words with magnetic letters.	5
Let the child choose a book for you to read aloud and read it.	10

Figure 12–8

SAMPLE PLAN #8 (45 MINUTES)	
Activity	Approximate Time in Minutes
Read aloud a favorite book or a new book.	5
Cut up the child's name (first, last, or both, depending on the child's knowledge and experience) and put the cut-up letters in an envelope. Ask the child to put together her name. Talk about the letters in the child's name.	10
Make a book with the child, using her name (example: "Latisha likes blue" or "Latisha likes to run"). Let the child write as much as she can, especially her name.	15
Read the child's book.	5
Do shared reading of a few familiar books.	10

Try these suggestions to increase your productivity:

- Plan for several sessions ahead of time so that it is easy to organize materials.

- Avoid interruptions—take care of conversations with others outside the time you spend with your partner and make sure your materials are ready.

- Right before the session, review your plan so that you are aware of everything you want to accomplish.

- Keep to your time schedule. If you have a good plan, all of the activities you have planned are important. Don't leave any out.

- Remember that the pace of the lesson is important. If you get "bogged down," it may not be effective for your partner. Keep things lively, moving from one activity to the next.

- If you have made a mistake, don't be afraid to adjust. At first, many volunteers tend to select books that are too hard for their partners. Additionally, they may introduce writing activities that are too hard. The child should never struggle, nor should she find the time she spends with the volunteer unpleasant. Not only will that make the child reluctant to try to read or write, it also will make the volunteering ineffective. So, if your partner is struggling, stop and revise the task. Read the book to her or choose an easier one. Write for her or show her how to write. Rely on your own sensitivity and good sense about what will help the child without taking the entire task away from her.

CREATING YOUR VOLUNTEER "TOOL KIT"

Many volunteers find it helpful to have a "kit" of materials they reserve for their work. It saves time and effort. Where can you keep your kit? The organization for which you volunteer might provide a safe place to store the kit, but if you use a car you might also store it in the trunk. Since you can use a simple plastic tub or box to store your materials, you can transport your kit daily or weekly. Any office supply store will give you a range of options for storage containers and materials. Figure 12–9 is an example of one tutor's tool kit.

How to pay for your kit

You might purchase this beginning tool kit yourself. Or, the university, business, or other agency that funds your work may provide it for you. As you look at the suggestions, you can make it as inexpensive as you like. For example, you can often obtain pens and markers without cost from businesses. You can borrow books from public libraries. The school or community center may donate paper. Yard sales are a good place to look for used books and all sorts of literacy materials.

Figure 12–9 *Volunteer Tool Kit*

The contents of your tool kit

We have found the following list of materials invaluable in our work with young children in literacy. Volunteers should make up their own tool kits to fit the unique demands of their particular jobs.

Materials may include:

- Some books that you can read to children.[1]

- Paper of various sizes and colors for book making.

- Pictures from catalogs and newspapers, organized in envelopes, that you can use for book making.

- Prestapled blank books for book making.

- Thin markers in dark colors for children to use as they write.

- Crayons and colored markers for children to draw pictures.

- Several glue sticks.

- Scissors.

[1]A list of paperback books that are available at most bookstores is included in Appendix B at the end of this book.

- A stapler.

- White Post-it tape (to cover mistakes). You can also use mailing labels, blank stickers, or small pieces of paper and glue.

- A notebook for recording plans and notes about children's responses.

A WORD ABOUT ROUTINES

You won't regret the advance time you spend organizing your materials and planning your sessions with children. Not only will your work be more successful but you will also enjoy it more. Think about the factors that enhance our daily lives. The routines we create free us to pay attention to what we value most. For example, many families establish customs and rituals around mealtimes. We can talk together and enjoy each others' company during mealtimes because we have routine ways of preparing and eating our meals.

You will create similar traditions and routines in your work with young children. Routines are simply comfortable, habitual ways of doing things. They make the child feel secure and free you both for learning conversations. For example, we described some ways to read aloud to children. You'll discover that reading aloud will quickly become a routine. The child will know your role and hers—to listen, notice, offer ideas, and so forth.

Routines free you from directing your partner's every move. And the efficient, warm interactions and routines that you create together will greatly enrich the child's experience.

TAKE NOTE

Consider your plans, the routines you've organized, and the materials you've collected. How do they help you as a successful literacy volunteer? Ask yourself:

◆ Is my commitment to volunteering fitting easily into my weekly schedule, and is the location I selected convenient, helping me fulfill my commitment?

◆ Are my materials organized and accessible so that I rarely need to think about them except to replenish them periodically?

◆ Am I writing some useful notes to document my work with my partner and to make effective plans for our next learning sessions?

◆ Are my plans workable—that is, am I able to complete the activities within my time frame and keep the pace of each learning session lively?

◆ Am I enjoying my work? (If you aren't, there is something wrong with the plan or the time allotment.)

A FINAL NOTE

In Chapter 2 we outlined ten ways of working with children:

- Develop children's language.

- Work with children as readers—read aloud, share reading together, and listen to them read.

- Introduce phonics—show children how letters, sounds, and words work.

- Work with children as writers—write for them, share writing together, and help them write.

- Make books to link reading and writing.

- Make connections with children's homes.

In the chapters of this book, we described each way of working and provided an array of suggestions. You are the decision maker. You can combine the ways of working or concentrate on one area, depending on the needs of your partner.

Don't forget to consider your own interests and strengths. Any of these approaches, if you do them well and enjoy your work with your partner, are beneficial. And, if you use the questions in the Take Note section at the end of each chapter together with your own powers of observation, you will see evidence that you are making a difference. You will know you are successful when your partner:

- Smiles and looks forward to working with you.

- Tries hard and shows you that she is pleased with her accomplishments.

- Can't wait to take home a new book or show her writing to her family.

- Can do a little more each day.

She will continually delight and surprise you with her new learning. These are the rewards of helping a child into literacy.

We live in an active society. There is much to do at work, at home, and in recreation. You have many choices competing for your precious free time. What you choose must be worth doing. By volunteering to work with young children, you become a member of a special group of people who are giving to the community. You also join a group of people committed to literacy education. You are a valuable partner in the education of young children. Our future lies in today's opportunities for children to learn. By offering your service, you increase that opportunity. Every child is capable and creative. Helping children realize their potential is a great privilege. It is work well worth doing.

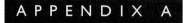

Books Too Good to Miss:
A Read-Aloud Selection

KINDERGARTEN

Aylesworth, J. 1993. *Old Black Fly.* New York: Holt.

Bayer, J. 1984. *A My Name Is Alice.* New York: Dial.

Campbell, R. 1982. *Dear Zoo.* New York: Simon and Schuster.

Carle, E. 1989. *The Very Hungry Caterpillar.* New York: Philomel.

Chocolate, D. 1996. *Kente Colors.* New York: Walker and Co.

de Paola, T. 1985. *Mother Goose.* New York: G. P. Putnam.

Emberley, R. 1993. *My House, Mi Casa.* Boston: Little, Brown.

Fleming, D. 1994. *Barnyard Banter.* New York: Henry Holt.

Fox, M. 1989. *Koala Lou.* New York: Gulliver.

Guarino, D. 1989. *Is Your Mama a Llama?* New York: Scholastic.

Harper, I., and B. Moser. 1994. *My Dog Rosie.* New York: The Blue Sky Press.

Hoban, T. 1981. *Twenty-Six Letters and Ninety-Nine Cents.* New York: Greenwillow.

Hutchins, P. 1968. *Rosie's Walk.* New York: Macmillan.

Jousse, B. M. 1991. *Mama, Do You Love Me?* San Francisco: Chronicle Books.

Kasza, K. 1987. *The Wolf's Chicken Stew.* New York: G. P. Putnam.

Keats, E. J. 1962. *The Snowy Day.* New York: Viking.

King, E. 1990. *The Pumpkin Patch.* New York: Dutton.

Kovalski, M. 1987. *The Wheels on the Bus.* Boston: Little, Brown.

Lewison, W. C. 1992. *Going to Sleep on the Farm.* New York: Dial.

Martin, B. Jr., and E. Carle. 1989. *Brown Bear, Brown Bear, What Do You See?* New York: Holt, Rinehart, and Winston.

McDonnell, F. 1994. *I Love Animals.* Cambridge, MA: Candlewick Press.

McKissack, P. C. 1986. *Flossie and the Fox.* New York: Dial.

Numeroff, L. J. 1985. *If You Give a Mouse a Cookie.* New York: HarperCollins.

Rockwell, A. 1997. *Show and Tell Day.* New York: HarperCollins.

Rosen, M. 1989. *We're Going on a Bear Hunt.* New York: Margaret K. McElderry Books.

Waber, B. 1972. *Ira Sleeps Over.* Boston: Houghton Mifflin.

Waddell, M. 1992. *Owl Babies.* Cambridge, MA: Candlewick Press.

Wells, R. 1973. *Noisy Nora.* New York: Dial.

Williams, S. 1989. *I Went Walking.* New York: Gulliver Books.

Young, R. 1992. *Golden Bear.* New York: Viking.

GRADE ONE

Ada, A. F. 1997. *Gathering the Sun.* New York: Lothrop, Lee and Shepard.

Alborough, J. 1992. *Where's My Teddy?* Cambridge, MA: Candlewick Press.

Barton, B. 1991. *The Three Bears.* New York: HarperCollins.

Brett, J. 1989. *The Mitten.* New York: G. P. Putnam.

Buckley, H., and J. Ormerod. 1994. *Grandfather and I.* New York: Lothrop, Lee and Shepard.

Bunting, E. 1994. *Flower Garden.* San Diego, CA: Harcourt Brace.

Cannon, J. 1993. *Stellaluna.* New York: Harcourt Brace.

Cherry, L. 1992. *The Great Kapok Tree.* New York: Gulliver Green.

Cousins, L. 1989. *The Little Dog Laughed.* New York: E. P. Dutton.

de Regniers, B. S. 1988. *Sing a Song of Popcorn.* New York: Scholastic.

Eastman, P. D. 1960. *Are You My Mother?* New York: Beginner Books.

Ehlert, L. 1989. *Eating the Alphabet*. New York: Harcourt Brace Jovanovich.

———. 1995. *Snowballs*. New York: Harcourt Brace.

Fleming, D. 1993. *In the Small, Small Pond*. New York: Henry Holt.

Florian, D. 1988. *A Carpenter*. New York: Greenwillow.

George, L. B. 1996. *Around the Pond: Who's Been Here?* New York: Greenwillow.

Hale, J. 1990. *Mary Had a Little Lamb*. New York: Scholastic.

Harper, J., and B. Moser. 1995. *My Cats Nick and Nora*. New York: The Blue Sky Press.

Henkes, K. 1990. *Julius the Baby of the World*. New York: Greenwillow.

———. 1995. *The Biggest Boy*. New York: Greenwillow.

Hoffman, M. 1991. *Amazing Grace*. New York: Dial.

Jousse, B. M. 1996. *I Love You the Purplest*. San Francisco: Chronicle Books.

Lindbergh, R. 1994. *What Is the Sun?* Cambridge, MA: Candlewick Press.

Polacco, P. 1992. *Chicken Sunday*. New York: Philomel.

Rylant, C. 1985. *The Relatives Came*. New York: Bradbury.

Sanders, M. 1995. *What's Your Name?* New York: Holiday House.

Stevens, J. 1995. *Tops and Bottoms*. San Diego: Harcourt Brace.

Waddell, M. 1991. *Farmer Duck*. Cambridge, MA: Candlewick Press.

Ward, C. 1988. *Cookie's Week*. New York: G. P. Putnam.

Yolen, J. 1987. *Owl Moon*. New York: Philomel.

GRADE TWO

Aardema, V. 1975. *Why Mosquitoes Buzz in People's Ears*. New York: Dial.

Begay, S. 1992. *Ma'ii and Cousin Horned Toad*. New York: Scholastic.

Brown, M. 1993. *Arthur's New Puppy*. Boston: Little, Brown.

Bunting, E. 1996. *Secret Place*. New York: Clarion.

Cherry, L. 1992. *A River Runs Wild*. New York: Gulliver Green.

Cooney, B. 1982. *Miss Rumphius*. New York: Viking.

Dorros, A. 1991. *Abuela*. New York: Dutton.

Fleming, D. 1996. *Where Once There Was a Wood*. New York: Henry Holt.

Flournoy, V. 1985. *The Patchwork Quilt*. New York: Dial.

Garza, C. L. 1990. *Family Pictures*. San Francisco: Children's Book Press.